SCATTERED COMICS
IS AN INDIE COMIC PUBLISHER
LOCATED IN SACRAMENTO,
CALIFORNIA. ESTABLISHED BY
JASON DUBE, SCATTERED COMICS
IS A INDEPENDENT COMIC BOOK
COMPANY THAT BRINGS TOGETHER
HIGH CALIBUR TALENTS AND
SELF-PUBLISHED CREATORS TO
PRODUCE FOR THE FANS COMIC BOOKS WITH
EYE-POPPING, STYLISTIC ARTWORK AND CAPTIVATING
AND MOVING STORYLINES.
UNDER THIS IMPRINT WE CREATE COMICS ABOUT THE
SUPERNATURAL, DREAMS,TEENAGE ROMANCE AND
ANGST, FANTASY AND HORROR. WE STRIVE TO TELL
STORIES THAT MEAN SOMETHING TO US.

ELI BEAIRD IS THE CREATOR
OF SLIM COMICS, HE HAS SPENT
THE LAST FEW YEARS WORKING
ON HIS SERIES OF GRAPHIC
NOVELS, FOLLOWING HIS DREAM
OF BEING A WELL-KNOWN
ILLUSTRATOR.
ELI IS KNOWN FOR HIS LOVABLE
CHARACTERS, CREATIVE UNIVERSE,
AND ADORABLE ART STYLE.

ACTION LAND

Story & Art by Eli Beaird

Slim Team
Assistant – Kelsey Beaird
Editors – Heidi Goldstein,
Jason Kassahn,
Sharman Bruni,
Allen Antoine
Continuity – Shay Haynes
Conception – Dustin Chance
Special Thanks –Jennifer Perez,
Matthew Gibson

SCATTERED COMICS
Jason Dube - President
Noel Serrato - Creative/Brand Director
Shane Will - Director of Operations
TC Fuller - Marketing

MAIN CHARACTER

FRANCHESCA SKY
AGE: 16
OVERACTIVE IMAGINATION,
NEW CARICATURE ARTIST
 FOR ACTION LAND. THE HERO.

IMPORTANT CHARACTERS

JEN
 AGE: 17
 LEAD
 AIRBRUSH
 RUMORED TO
 BE THE CUTEST
 WORKER AT
 THE PARK.
 FOURTH SEASON.

ALEXIS
 AGE: 19
 LEAD
 AIRBRUSH/
 CARICATURES
 SPECIALIZES
 IN PARK
 REGULATIONS,
 TOTAL NERD.
 THIRD SEASON.

CARICATURE ARTISTS

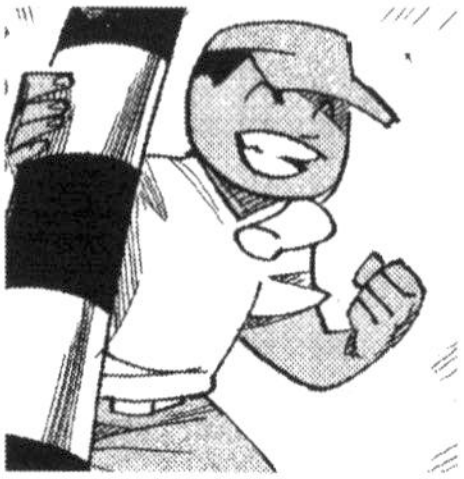

BRANDON
AGE: 24
CARICATURES
LEAD
LOVES TO PAINT ANIMALS.
FOURTH SEASON.

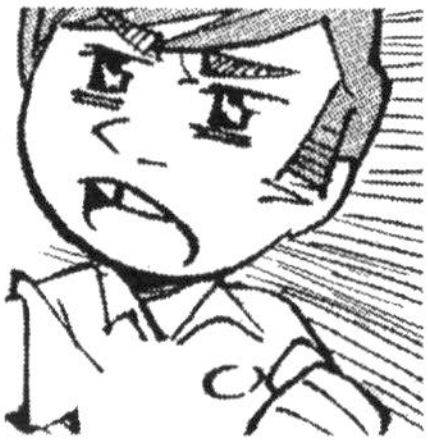

DUSTIN
AGE: 18
HOST
CARICATURES
SARCASTIC MOST OF THE TIME.
THIRD SEASON.

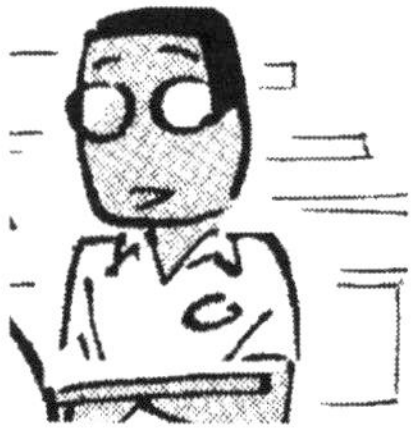

ELI
AGE: 18
HOST
CARICATURES
DUSTIN'S BEST FRIEND/RIVAL
OF 5 YEARS.
FIFTH SEASON.

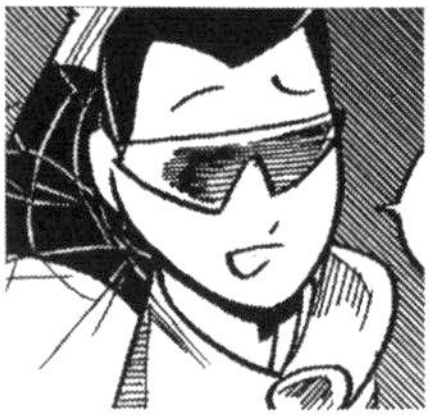

DAVID
AGE: UNKNOWN
HOST
CARICATURES BELIEVED
TO BE THE STRONGEST
ARTIST IN ACTION LAND.
TENTH SEASON.

ACTION LAND
BOOK 1

first day

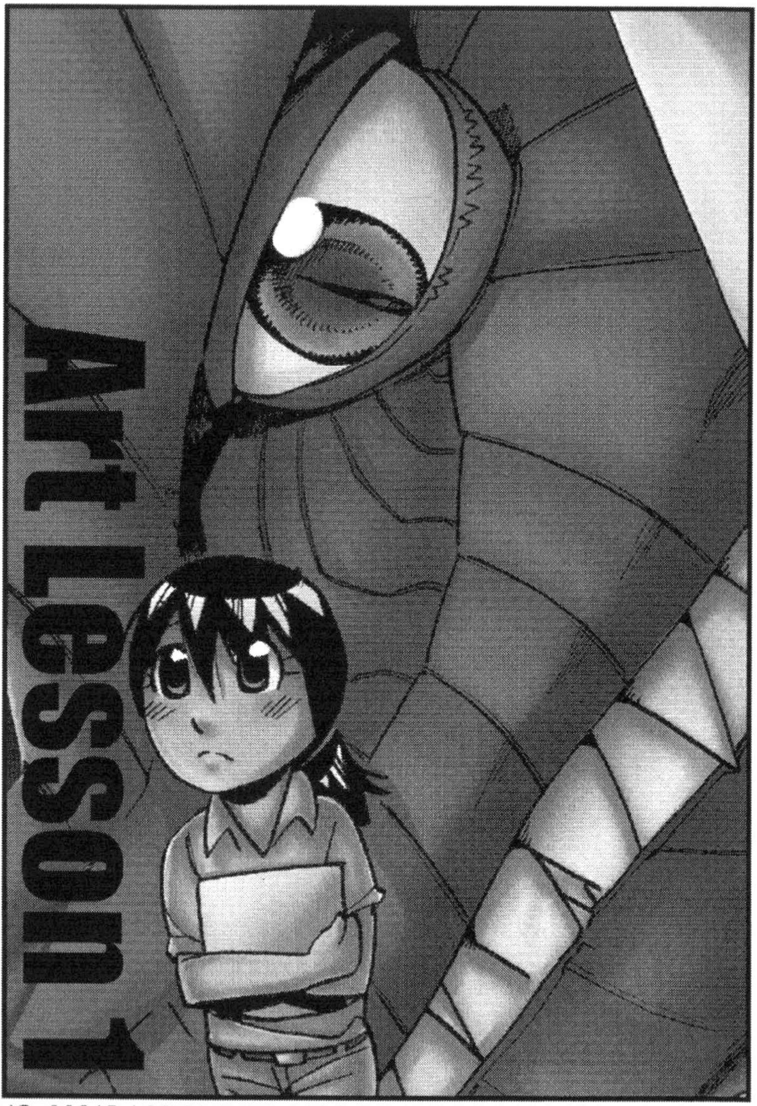
Art Lesson 1

NO GREAT ARTIST EVER SEES THINGS AS THEY REALLY ARE.
IF HE DID, HE WOULD CEASE TO BE AN ARTIST.
-OSCAR WILDE

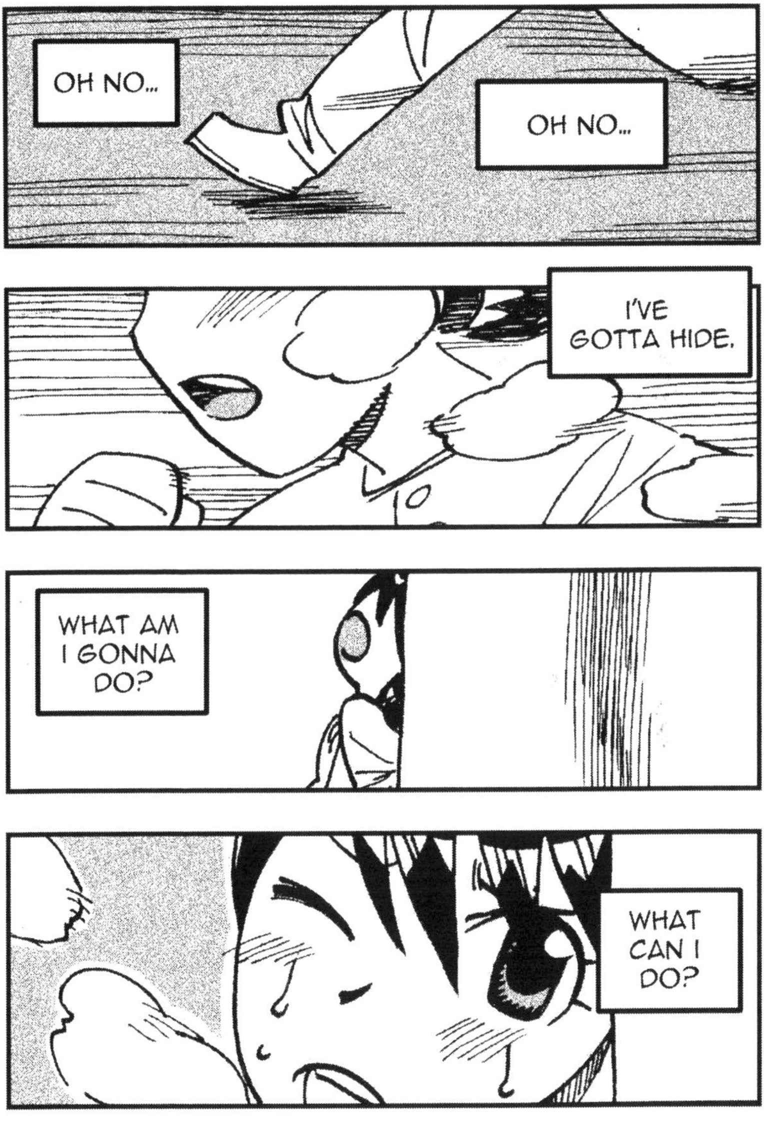
OH NO...
OH NO...
I'VE GOTTA HIDE.
WHAT AM I GONNA DO?
WHAT CAN I DO?

I CAN'T GO THROUGH THIS AGAIN....
PLEASE GO AWAY...
DON'T FIND ME.
...?!

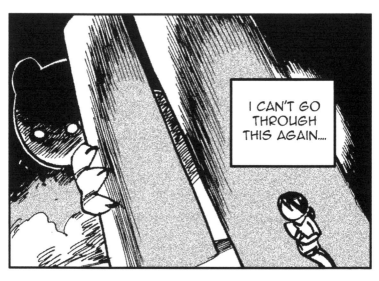

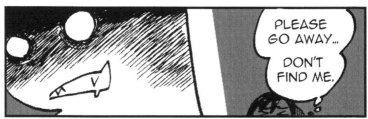

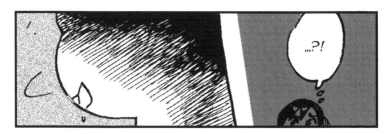

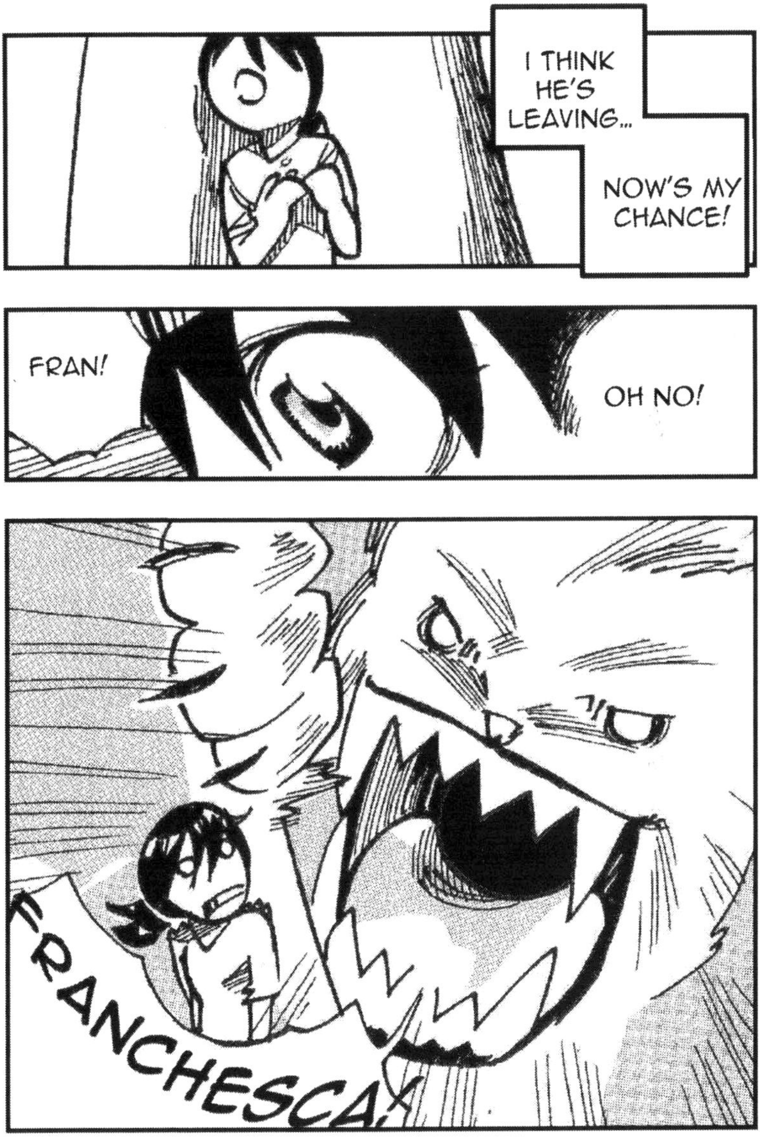
I THINK HE'S LEAVING...
NOW'S MY CHANCE!
FRAN!
OH NO!
FRANCHESCA!

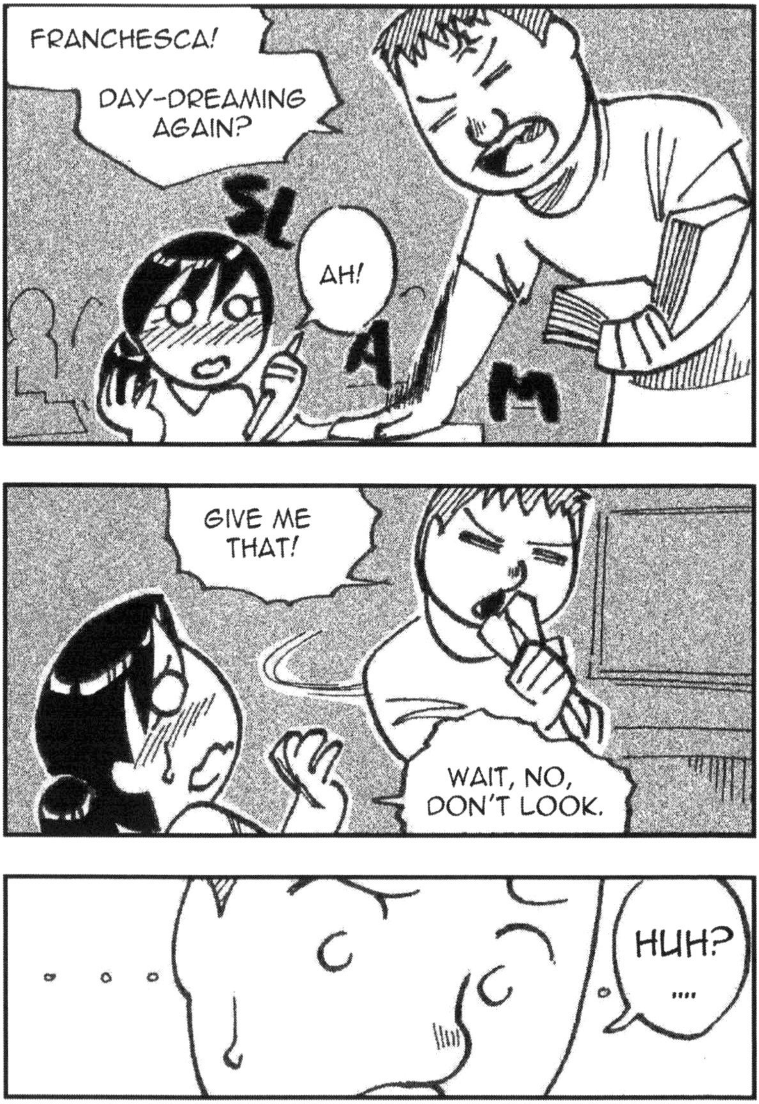
FRANCHESCA!
DAY-DREAMING AGAIN?
SLAM
AH!
GIVE ME THAT!
WAIT, NO, DON'T LOOK.
HUH?
....

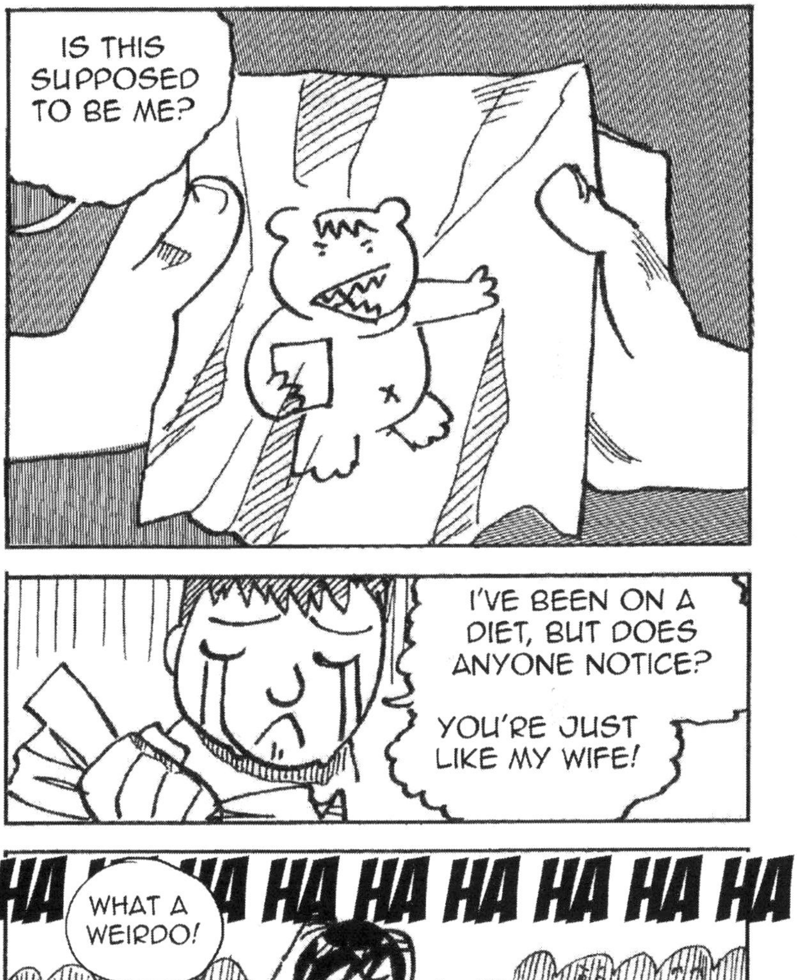
IS THIS SUPPOSED TO BE ME?
I'VE BEEN ON A DIET, BUT DOES ANYONE NOTICE?
YOU'RE JUST LIKE MY WIFE!
HA HA HA HA HA HA HA HA
WHAT A WEIRDO!
...NO!

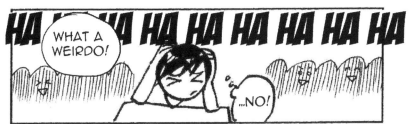

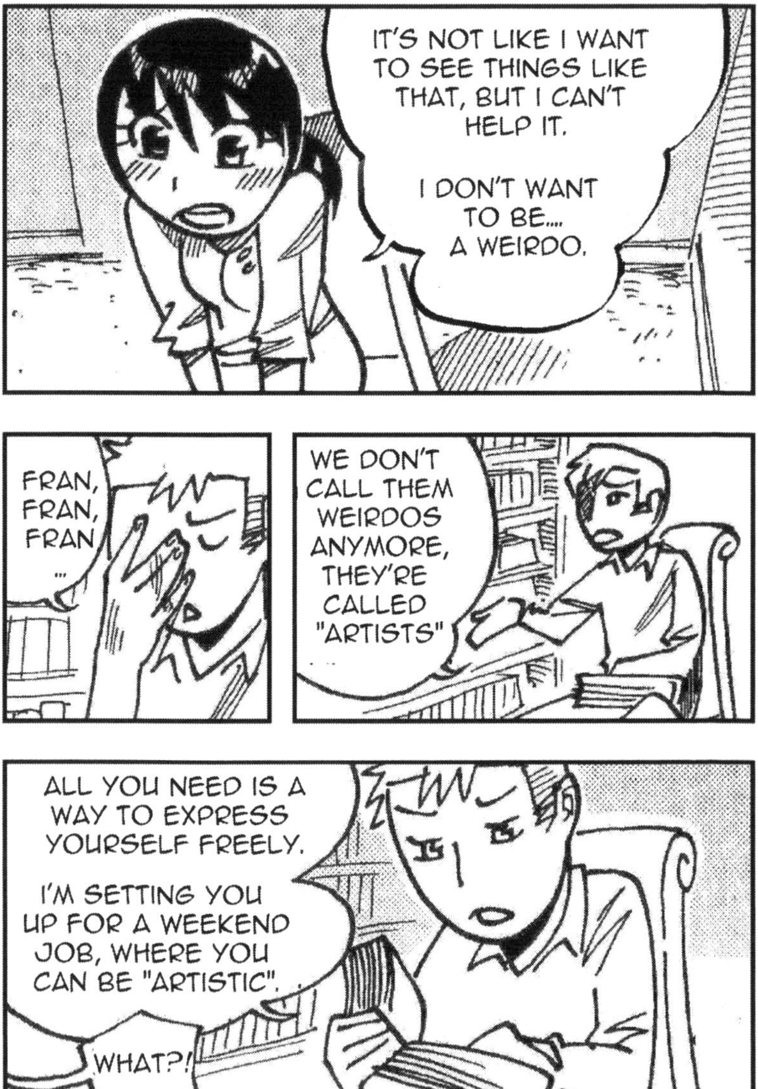
IT'S NOT LIKE I WANT TO SEE THINGS LIKE THAT, BUT I CAN'T HELP IT.
I DON'T WANT TO BE.... A WEIRDO.
FRAN, FRAN, FRAN ...
WE DON'T CALL THEM WEIRDOS ANYMORE, THEY'RE CALLED "ARTISTS"
ALL YOU NEED IS A WAY TO EXPRESS YOURSELF FREELY.
I'M SETTING YOU UP FOR A WEEKEND JOB, WHERE YOU CAN BE "ARTISTIC".
WHAT?!

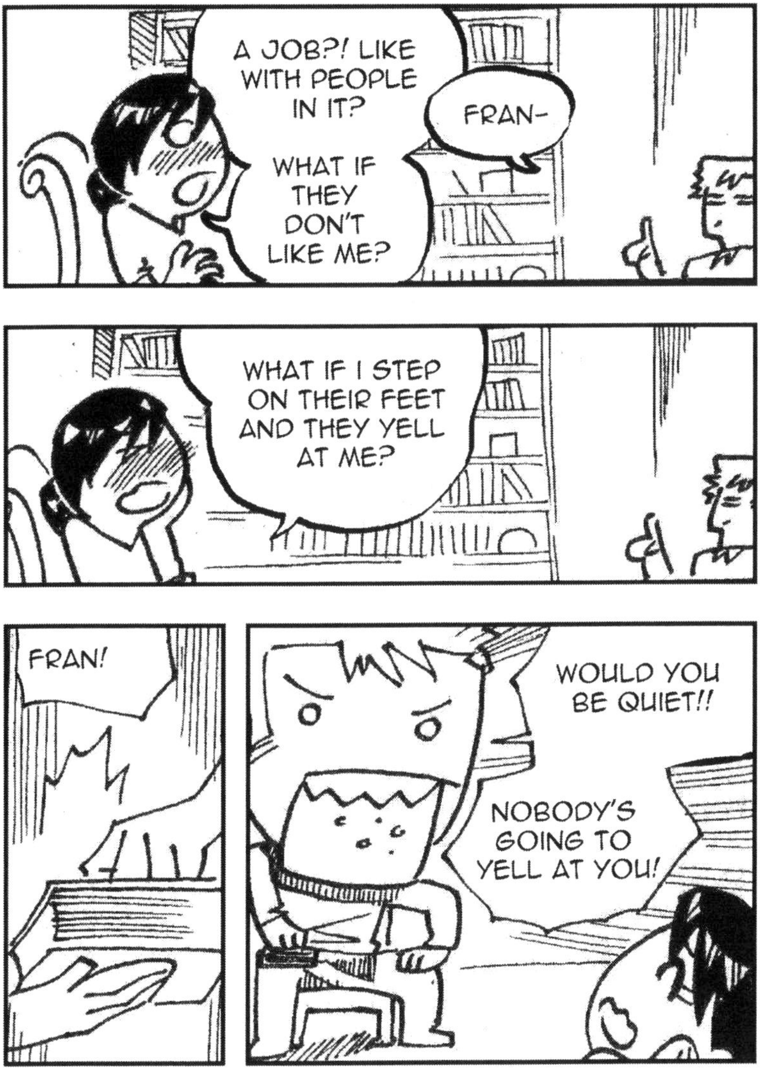
A JOB?! LIKE WITH PEOPLE IN IT?
WHAT IF THEY DON'T LIKE ME?
FRAN-
WHAT IF I STEP ON THEIR FEET AND THEY YELL AT ME?
FRAN!
WOULD YOU BE QUIET!!
NOBODY'S GOING TO YELL AT YOU!

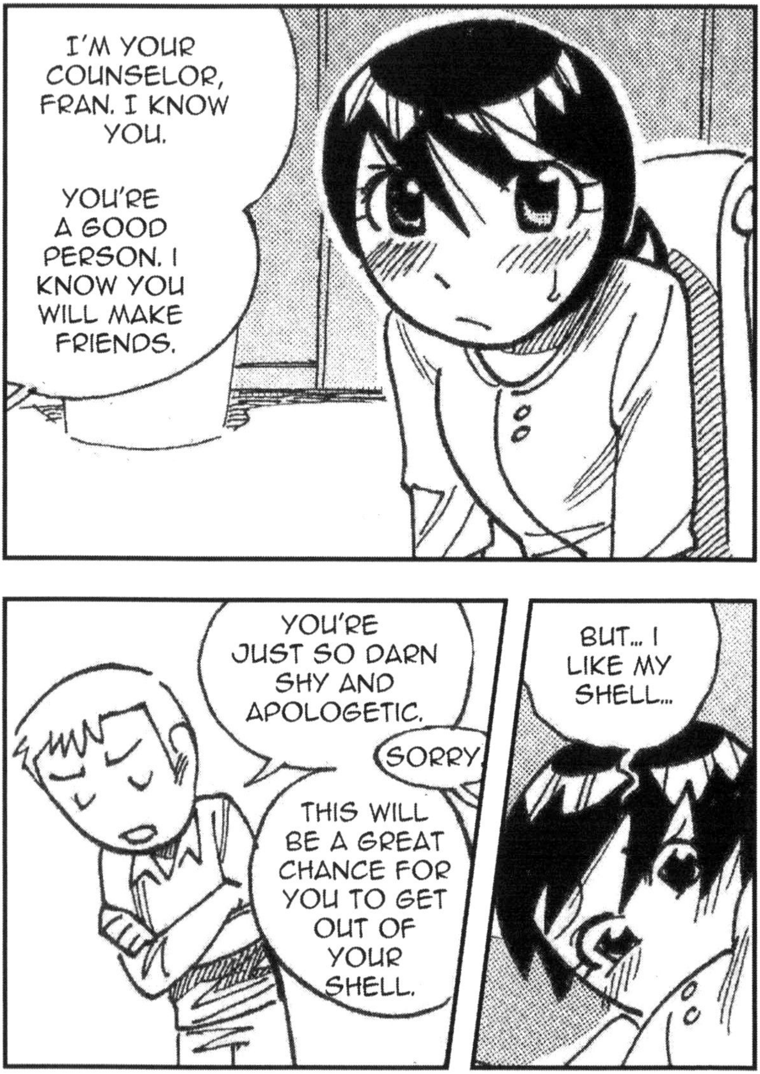
I'M YOUR COUNSELOR, FRAN. I KNOW YOU.
YOU'RE A GOOD PERSON. I KNOW YOU WILL MAKE FRIENDS.
YOU'RE JUST SO DARN SHY AND APOLOGETIC.
SORRY.
THIS WILL BE A GREAT CHANCE FOR YOU TO GET OUT OF YOUR SHELL.
BUT... I LIKE MY SHELL...

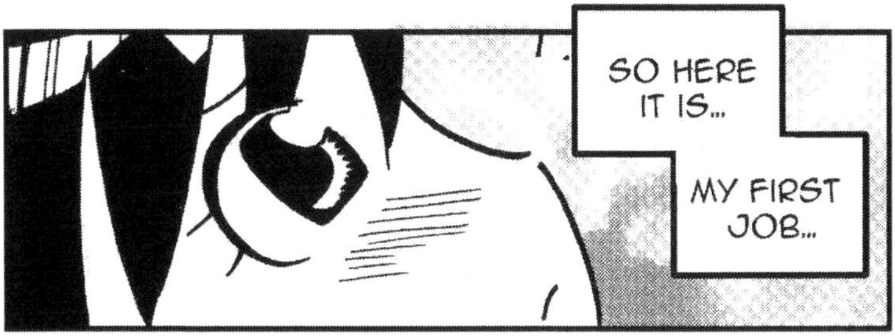
SO HERE IT IS...
MY FIRST JOB...

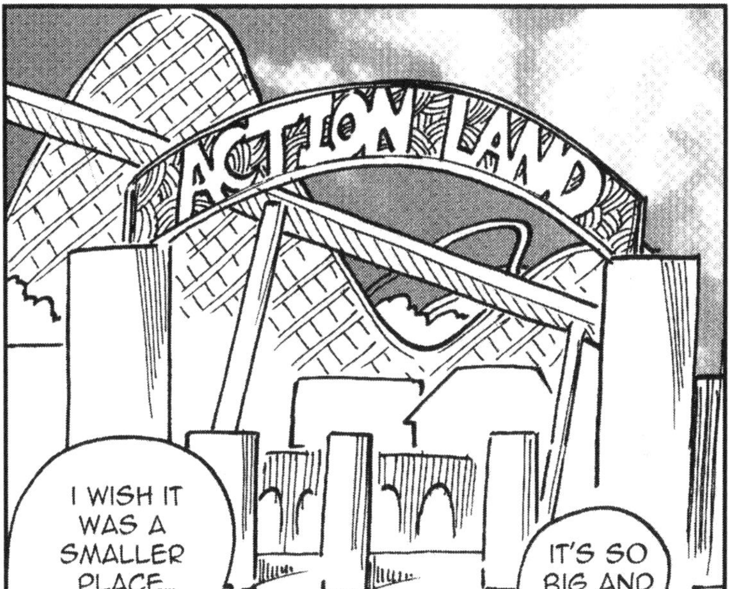
ACTION LAND
I WISH IT WAS A SMALLER PLACE...
IT'S SO BIG AND OLD....

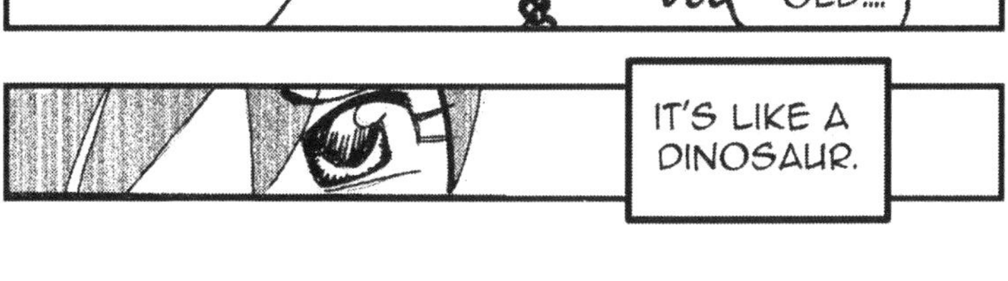
IT'S LIKE A DINOSAUR.

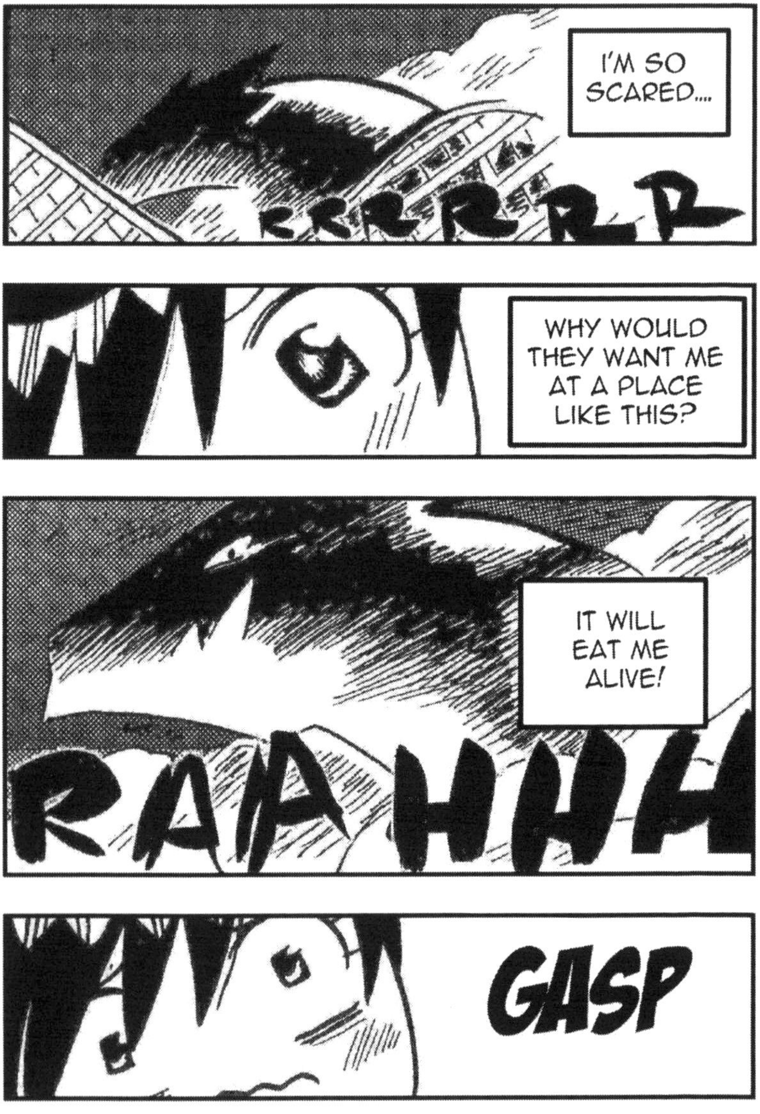
I'M SO SCARED....
RRRRRR
WHY WOULD THEY WANT ME AT A PLACE LIKE THIS?
IT WILL EAT ME ALIVE!
RAAHHH
GASP

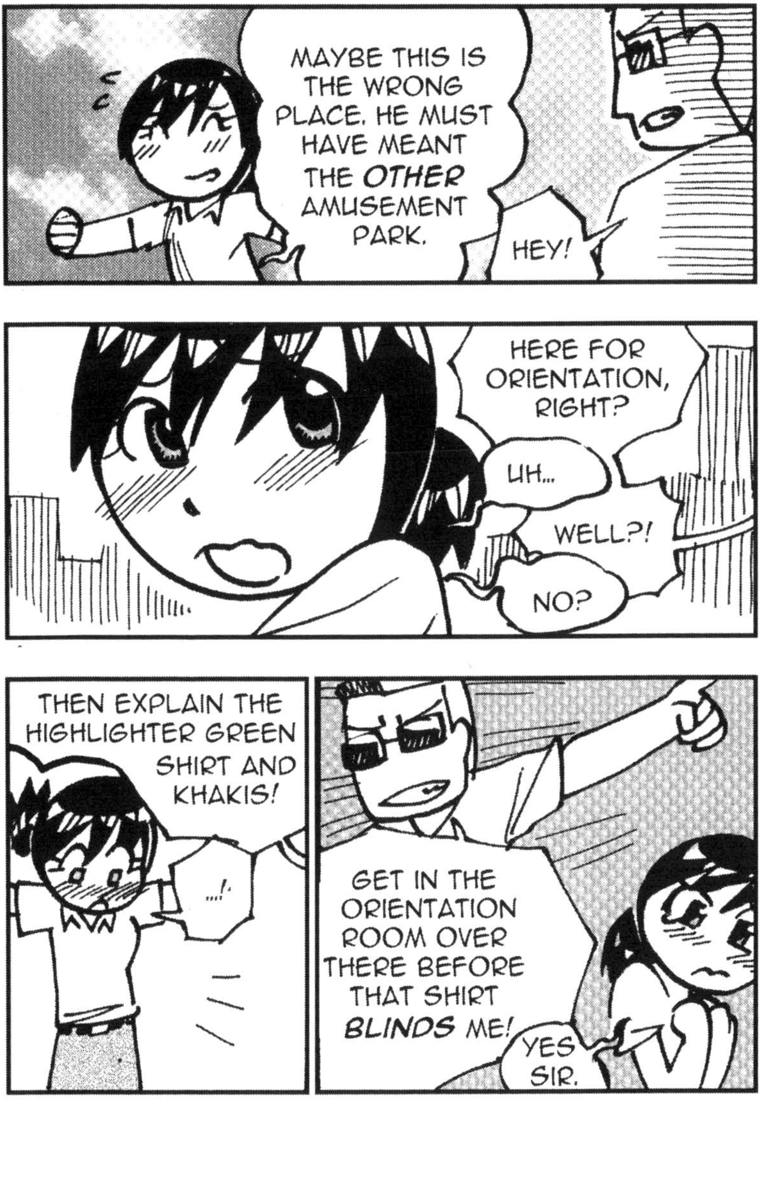
MAYBE THIS IS THE WRONG PLACE. HE MUST HAVE MEANT THE *OTHER* AMUSEMENT PARK.
HEY!
HERE FOR ORIENTATION, RIGHT?
UH...
WELL?!
NO?
THEN EXPLAIN THE HIGHLIGHTER GREEN SHIRT AND KHAKIS!
...!
GET IN THE ORIENTATION ROOM OVER THERE BEFORE THAT SHIRT *BLINDS* ME!
YES SIR.

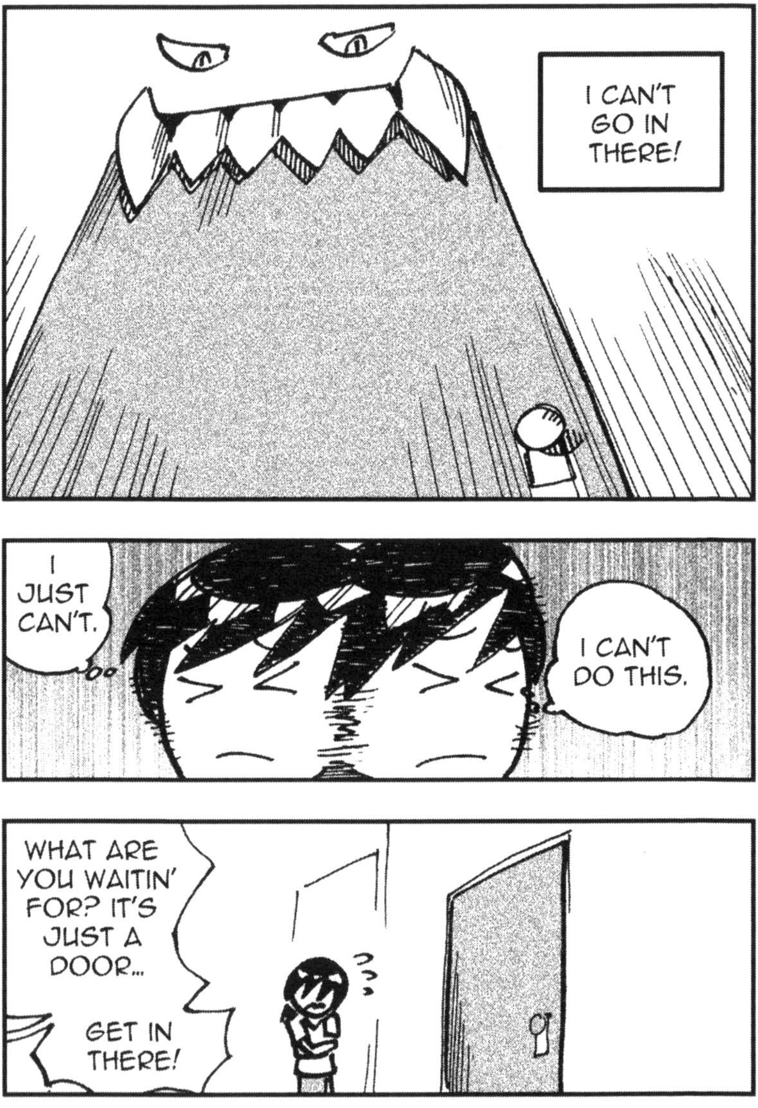
I CAN'T GO IN THERE!
I JUST CAN'T.
I CAN'T DO THIS.
WHAT ARE YOU WAITIN' FOR? IT'S JUST A DOOR...
GET IN THERE!

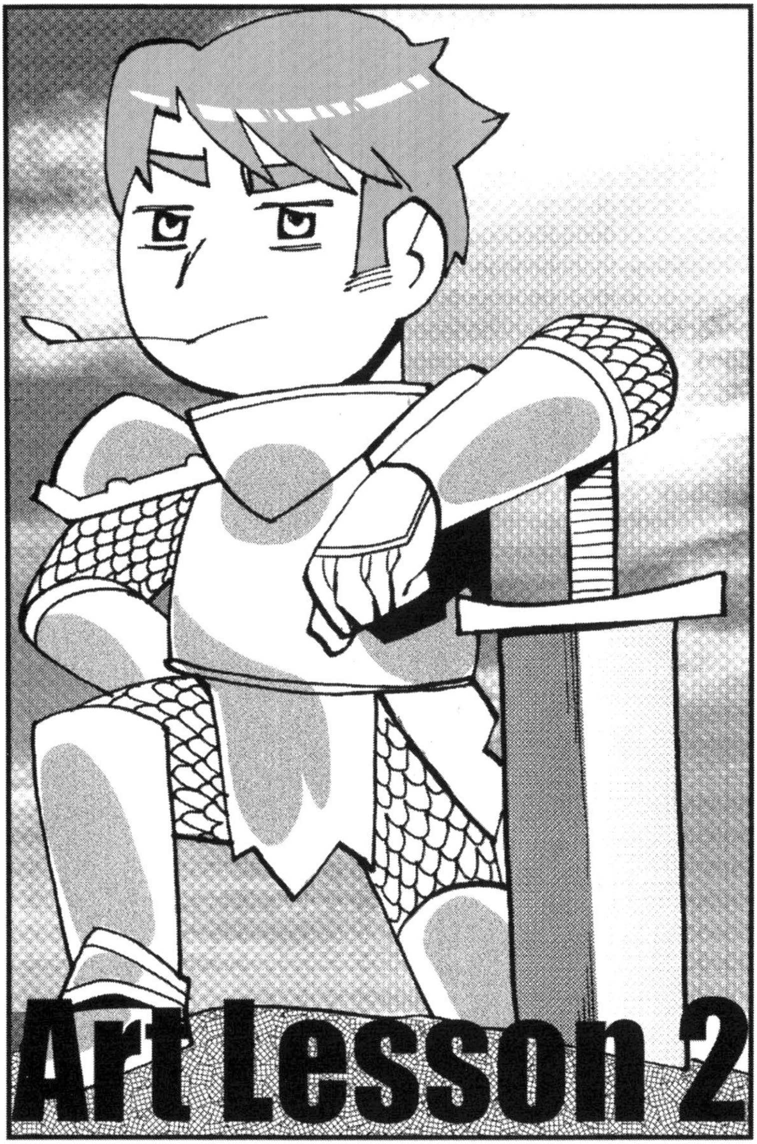
Art Lesson 2

THE AIM OF ART IS TO REPRESENT NOT THE OUTWARD APPEARANCE OF THINGS, BUT THEIR INWARD SIGNIFICANCE.
-ARISTOTLE

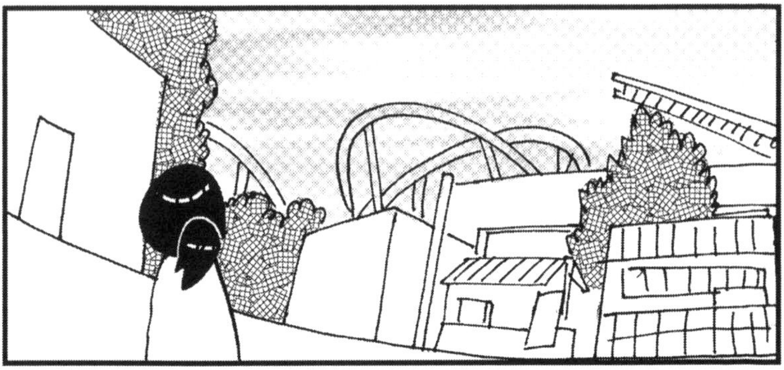

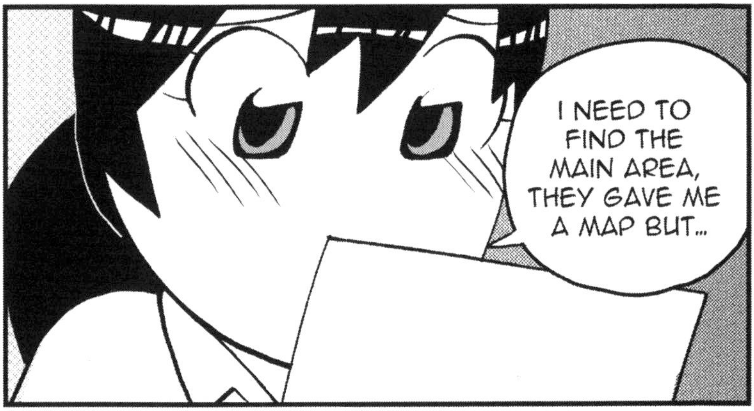
I NEED TO FIND THE MAIN AREA, THEY GAVE ME A MAP BUT...

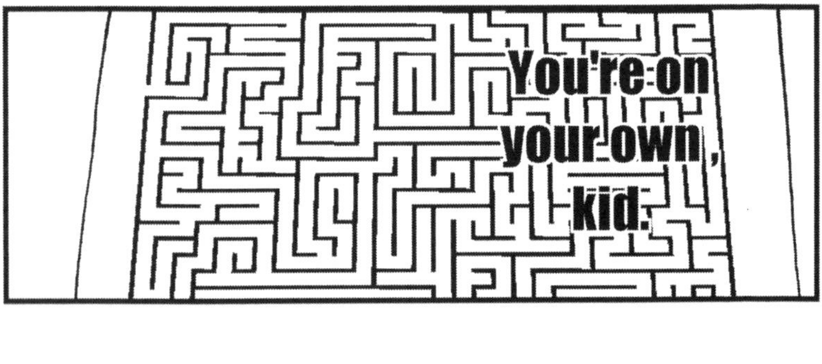
You're on your own, kid.

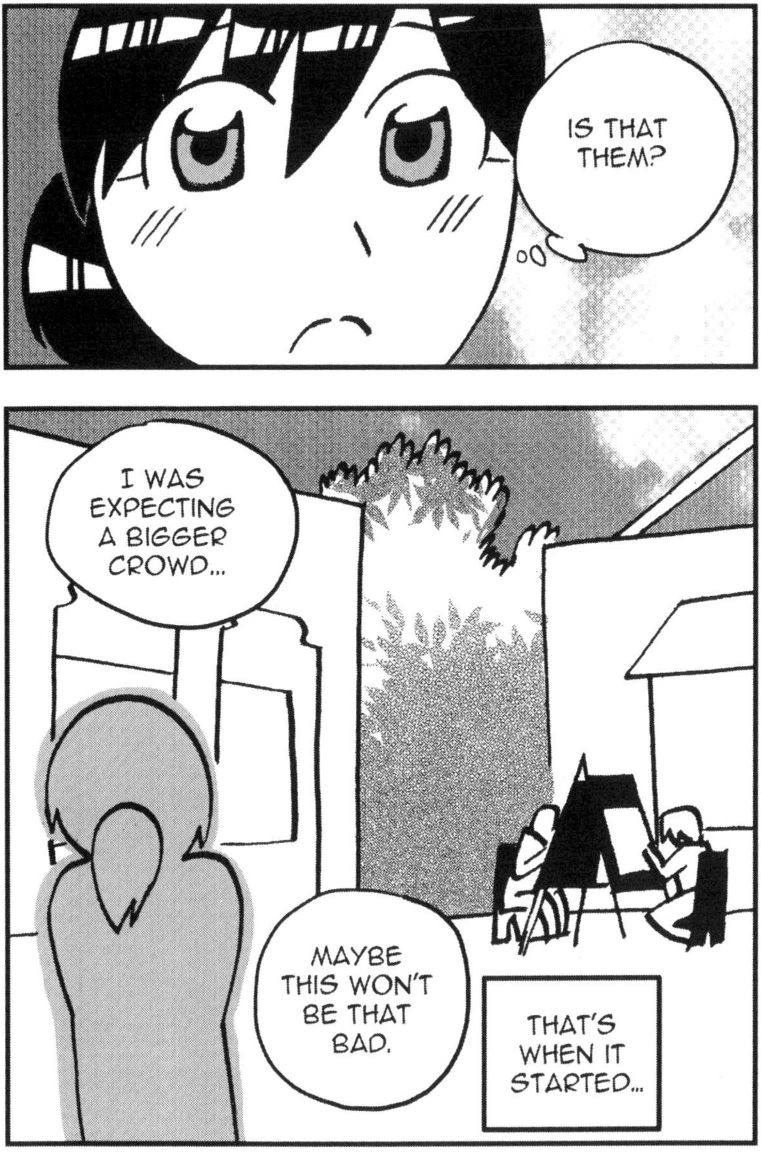
IS THAT THEM?
I WAS EXPECTING A BIGGER CROWD...
MAYBE THIS WON'T BE THAT BAD.
THAT'S WHEN IT STARTED...

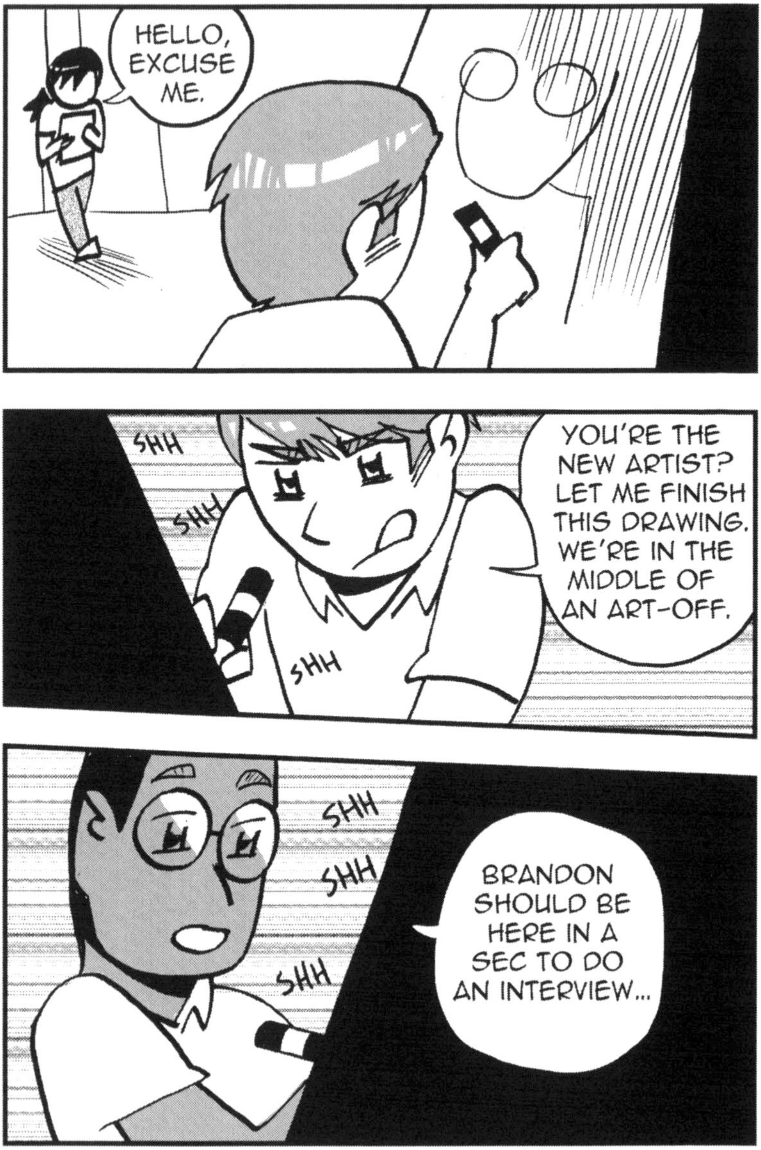
HELLO, EXCUSE ME.
SHH
SHH
YOU'RE THE NEW ARTIST? LET ME FINISH THIS DRAWING. WE'RE IN THE MIDDLE OF AN ART-OFF.
SHH
SHH
SHH
SHH
BRANDON SHOULD BE HERE IN A SEC TO DO AN INTERVIEW...

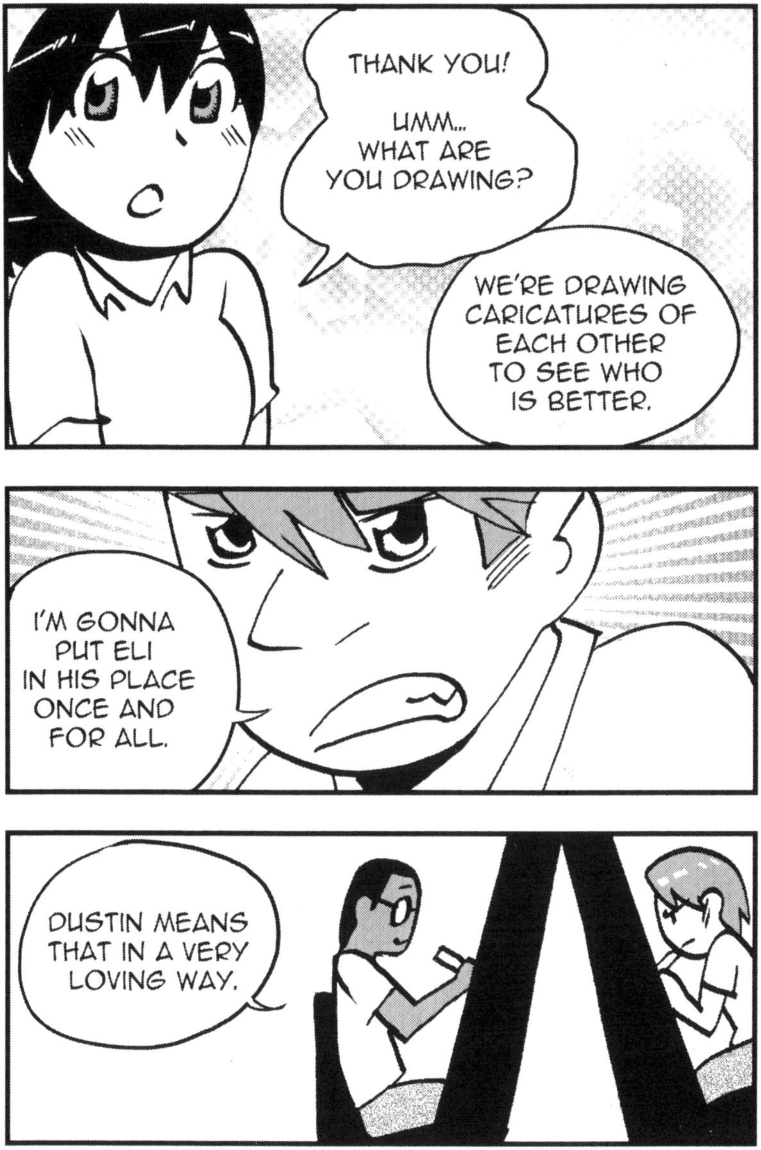
THANK YOU!
UMM... WHAT ARE YOU DRAWING?
WE'RE DRAWING CARICATURES OF EACH OTHER TO SEE WHO IS BETTER.
I'M GONNA PUT ELI IN HIS PLACE ONCE AND FOR ALL.
DUSTIN MEANS THAT IN A VERY LOVING WAY.

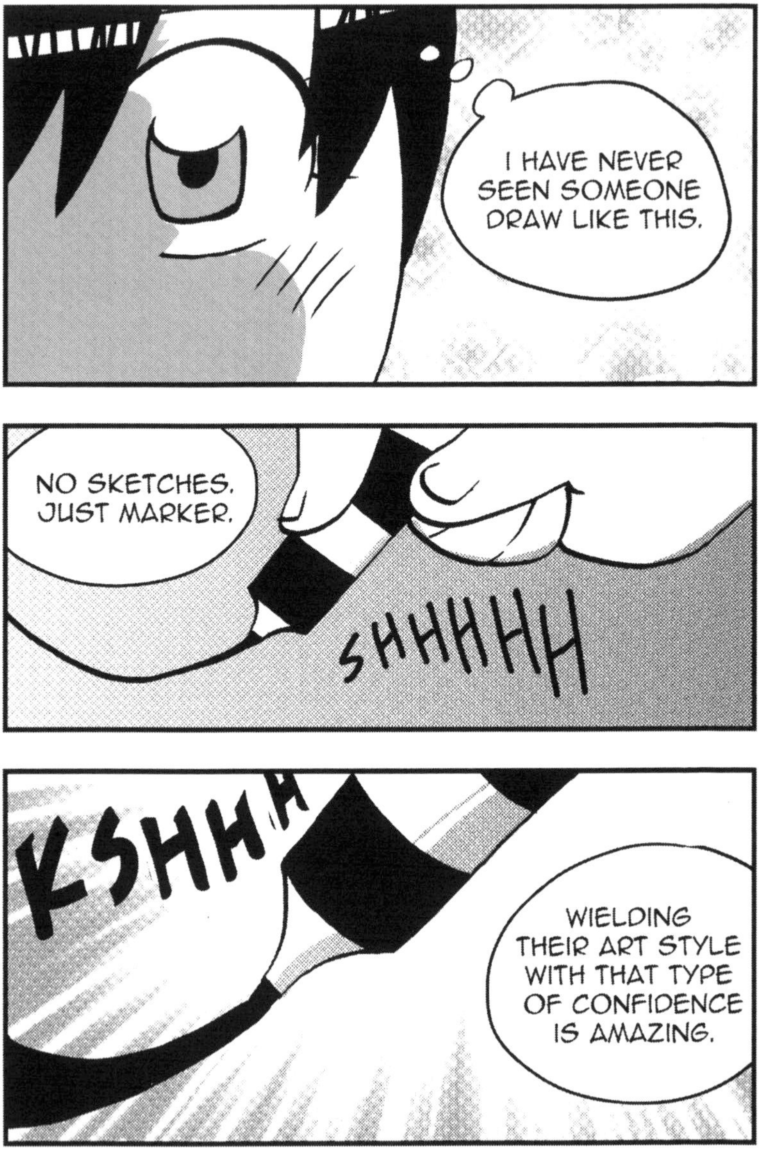
I HAVE NEVER SEEN SOMEONE DRAW LIKE THIS.
NO SKETCHES. JUST MARKER.
SHHHHHH
KSHHA
WIELDING THEIR ART STYLE WITH THAT TYPE OF CONFIDENCE IS AMAZING.

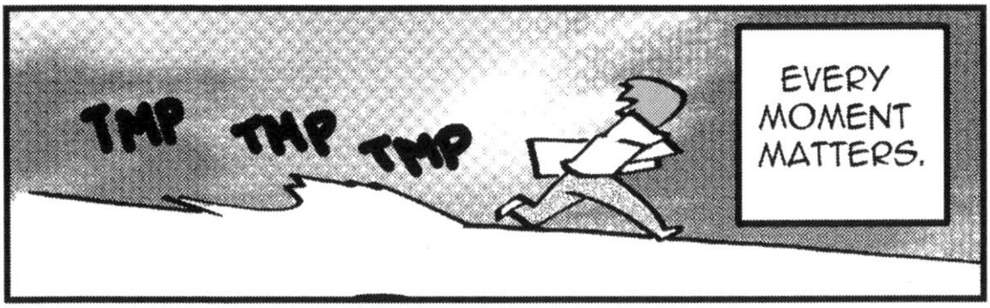
TMP THP TMP
EVERY MOMENT MATTERS.

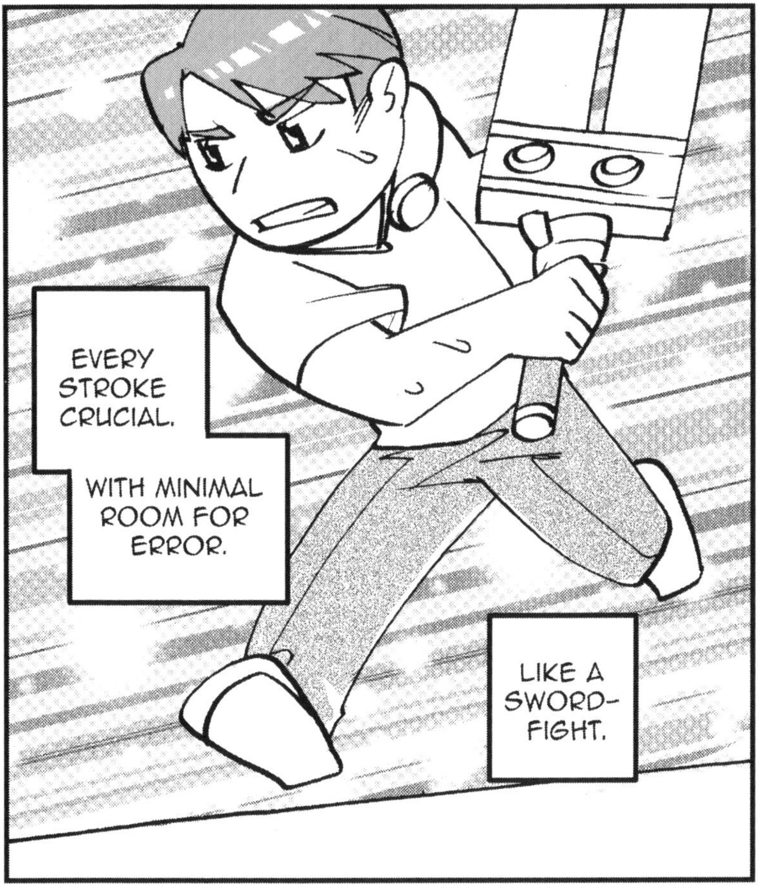
EVERY STROKE CRUCIAL.
WITH MINIMAL ROOM FOR ERROR.
LIKE A SWORD-FIGHT.

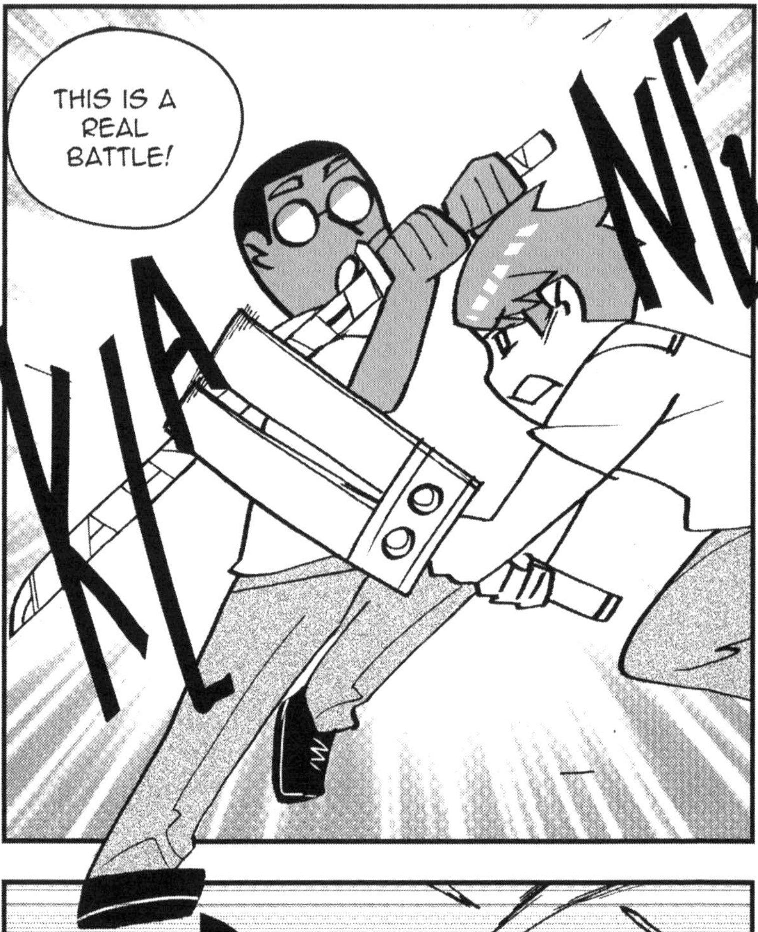
THIS IS A REAL BATTLE!
KLANG

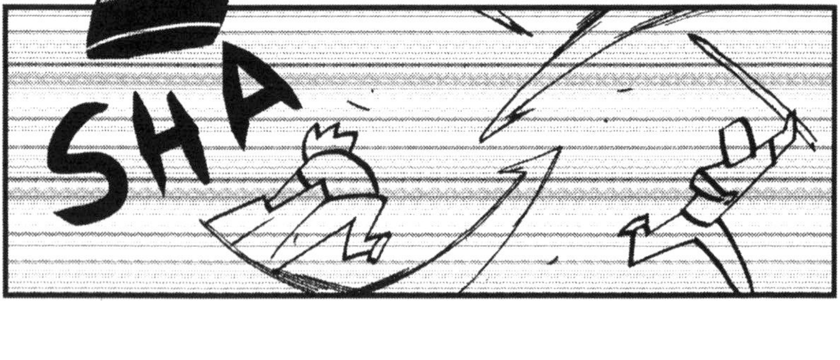
SHA

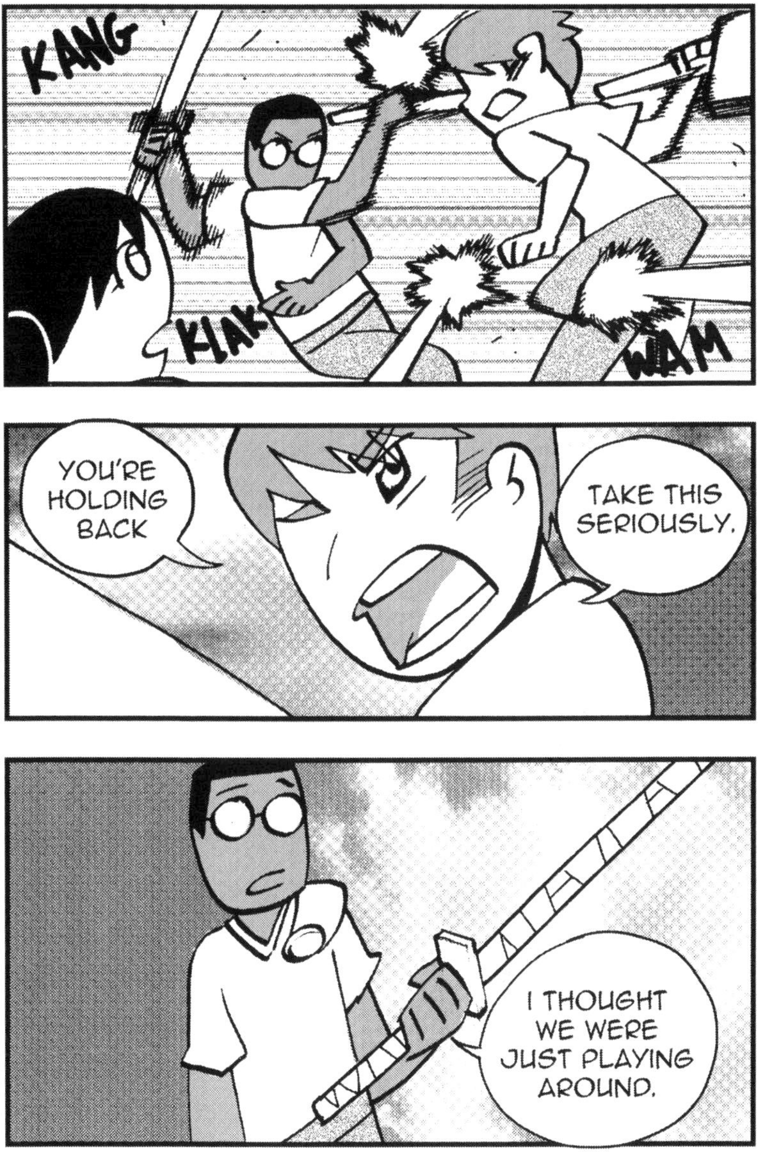
KANG
KIAK
WAM
YOU'RE HOLDING BACK
TAKE THIS SERIOUSLY.
I THOUGHT WE WERE JUST PLAYING AROUND.

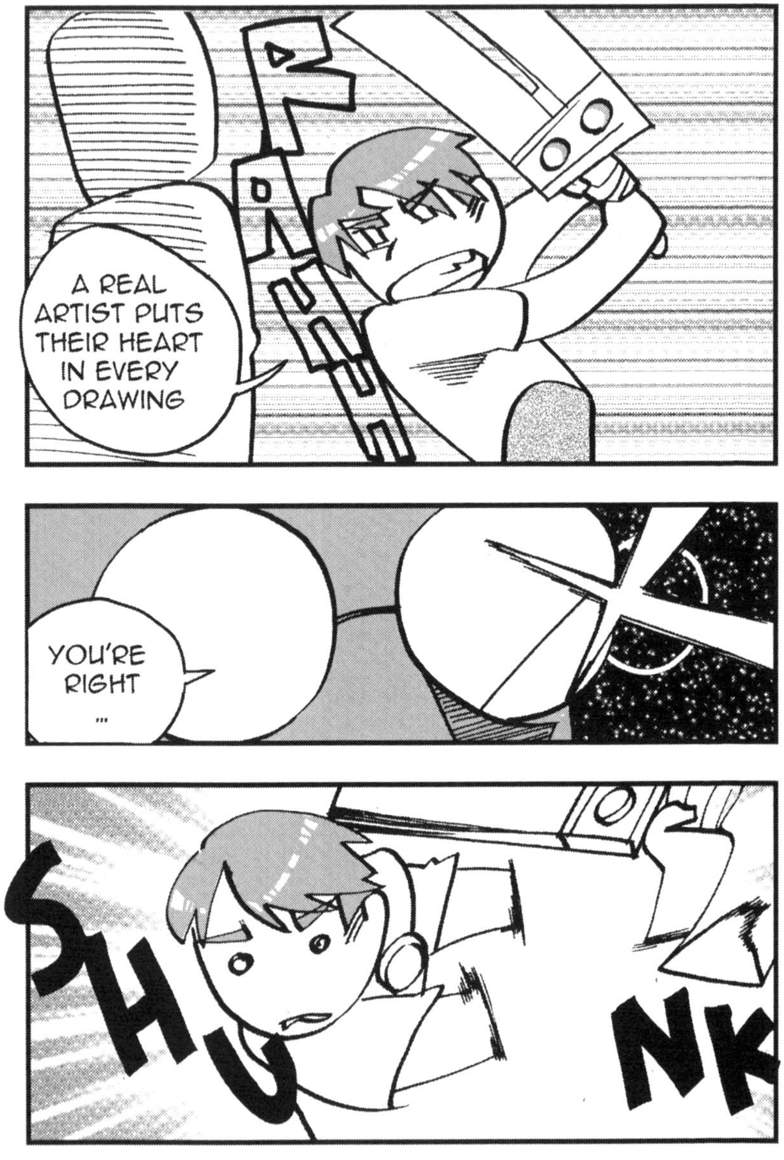
A REAL ARTIST PUTS THEIR HEART IN EVERY DRAWING
YOU'RE RIGHT ...
SHUNK

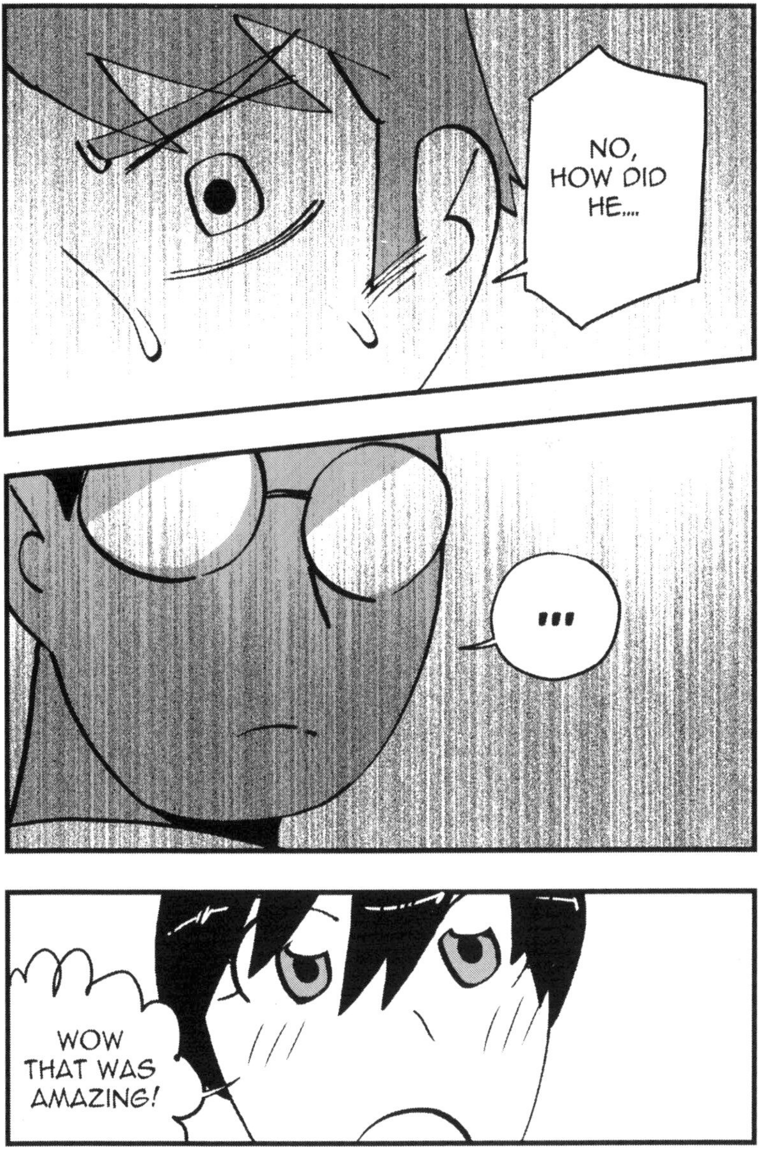
NO, HOW DID HE....
...
WOW THAT WAS AMAZING!

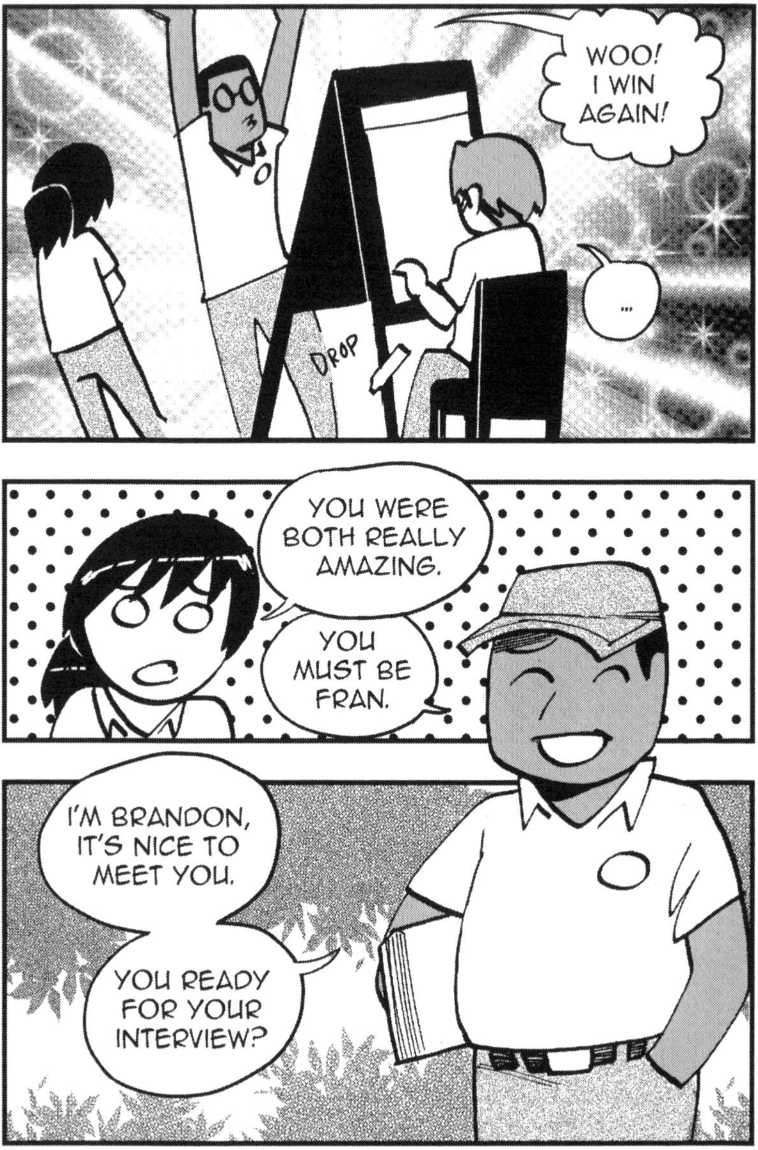
WOO! I WIN AGAIN!
DROP
...
YOU WERE BOTH REALLY AMAZING.
YOU MUST BE FRAN.
I'M BRANDON, IT'S NICE TO MEET YOU.
YOU READY FOR YOUR INTERVIEW?

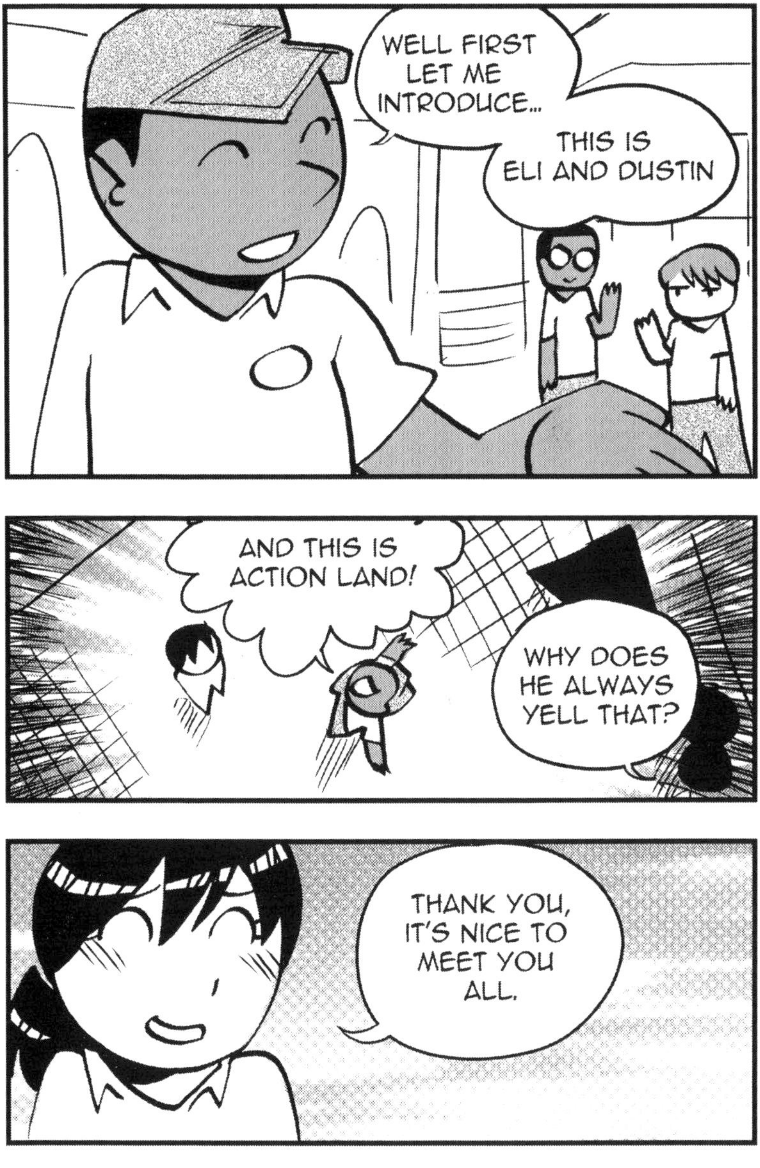
WELL FIRST LET ME INTRODUCE...
THIS IS ELI AND DUSTIN
AND THIS IS ACTION LAND!
WHY DOES HE ALWAYS YELL THAT?
THANK YOU, IT'S NICE TO MEET YOU ALL.

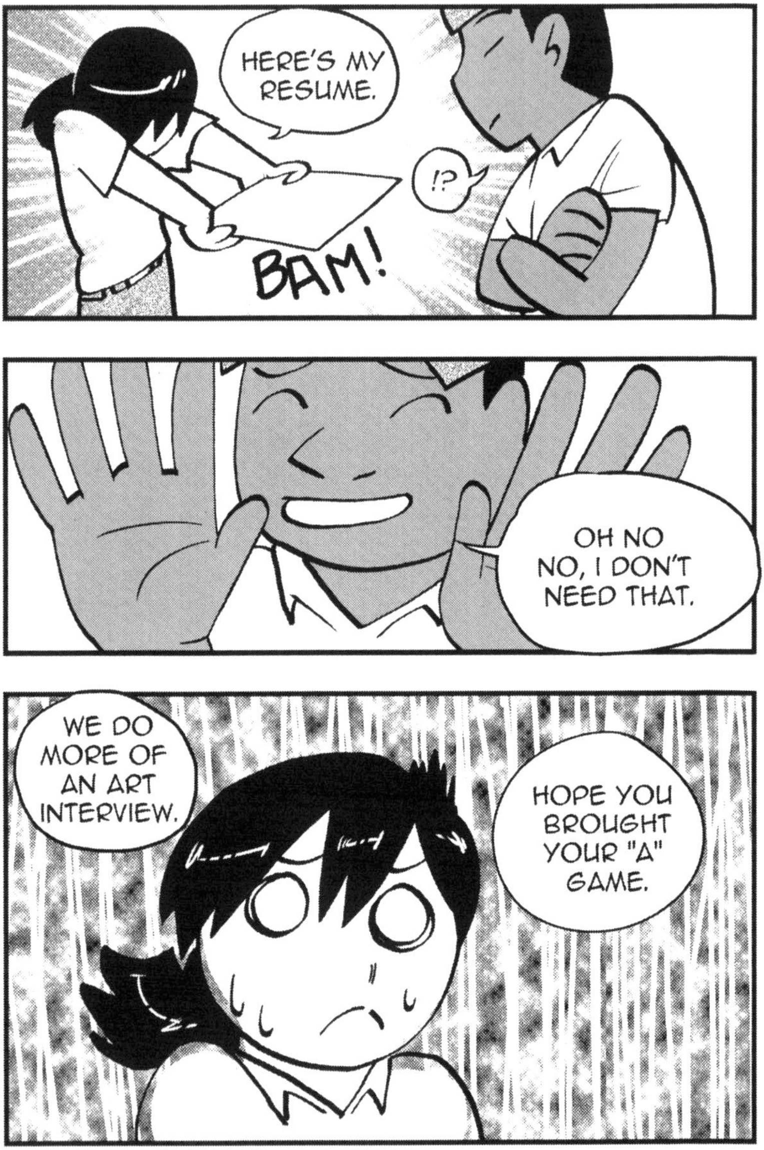
HERE'S MY RESUME.
!?
BAM!
OH NO NO, I DON'T NEED THAT.
WE DO MORE OF AN ART INTERVIEW.
HOPE YOU BROUGHT YOUR "A" GAME.

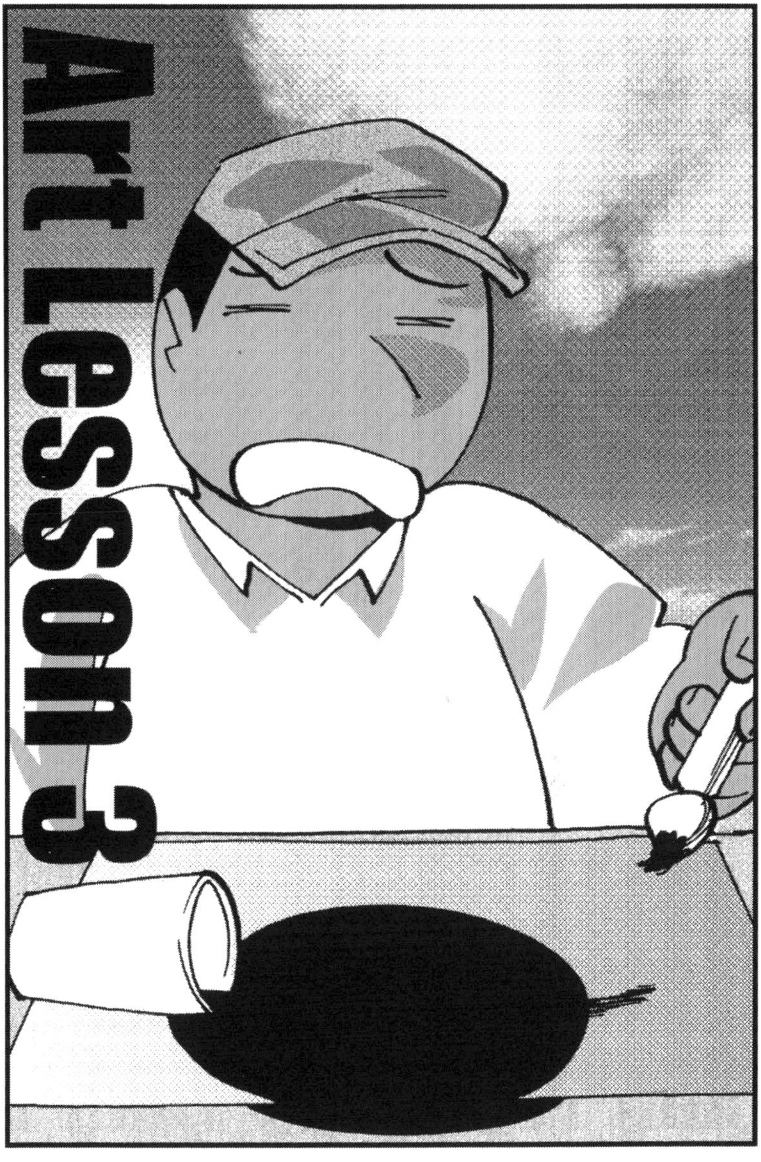
Art Lesson 3

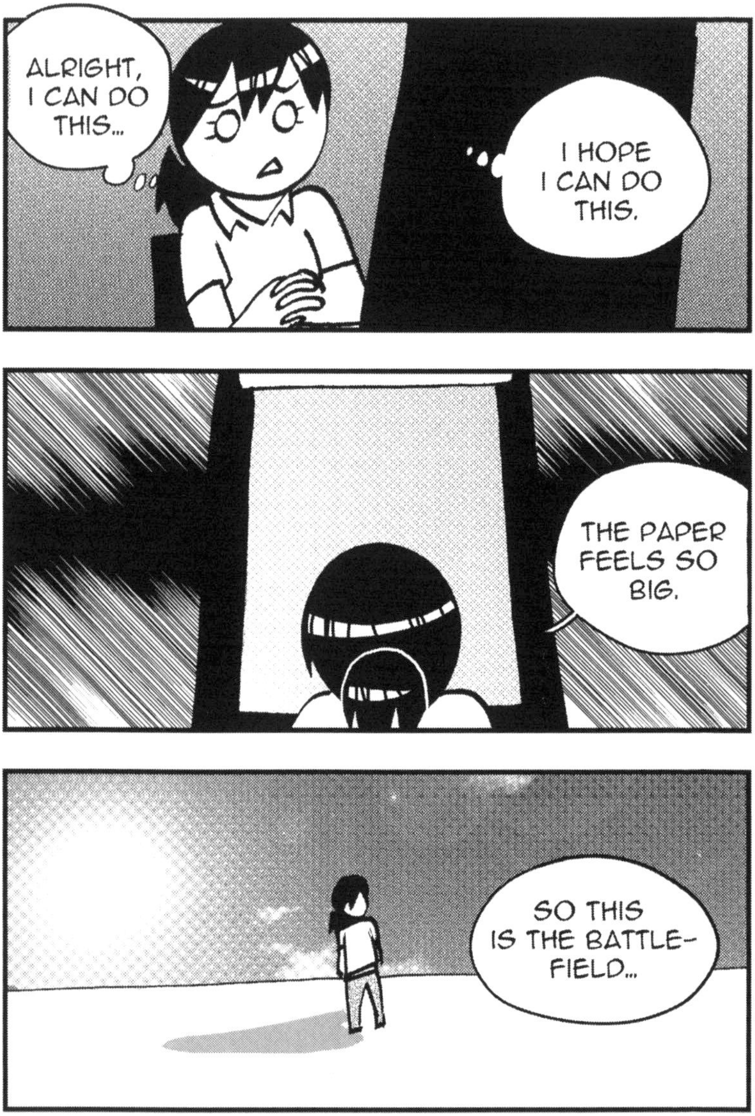
ALRIGHT, I CAN DO THIS...
I HOPE I CAN DO THIS.
THE PAPER FEELS SO BIG.
SO THIS IS THE BATTLE-FIELD...

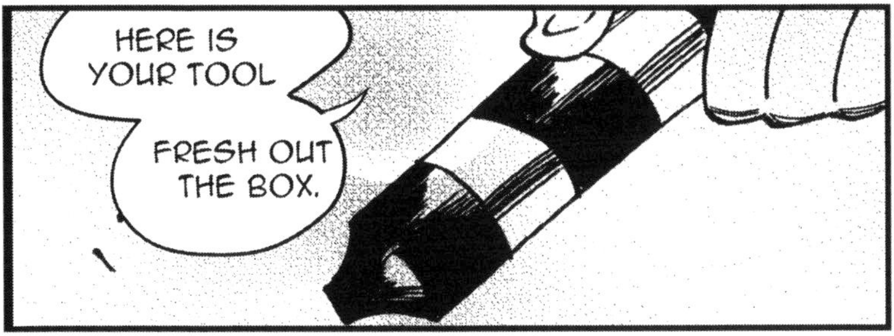
HERE IS YOUR TOOL
FRESH OUT THE BOX.
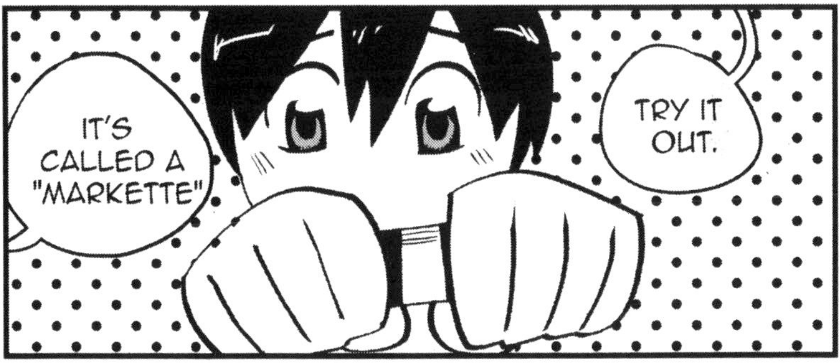
IT'S CALLED A "MARKETTE"
TRY IT OUT.
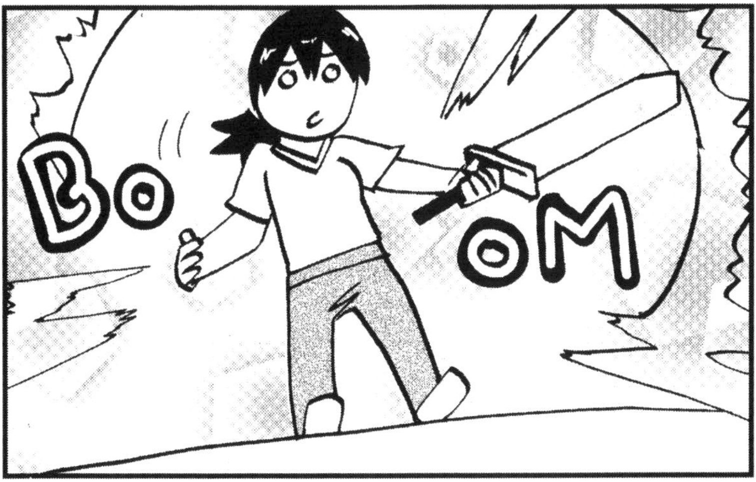
BOOM

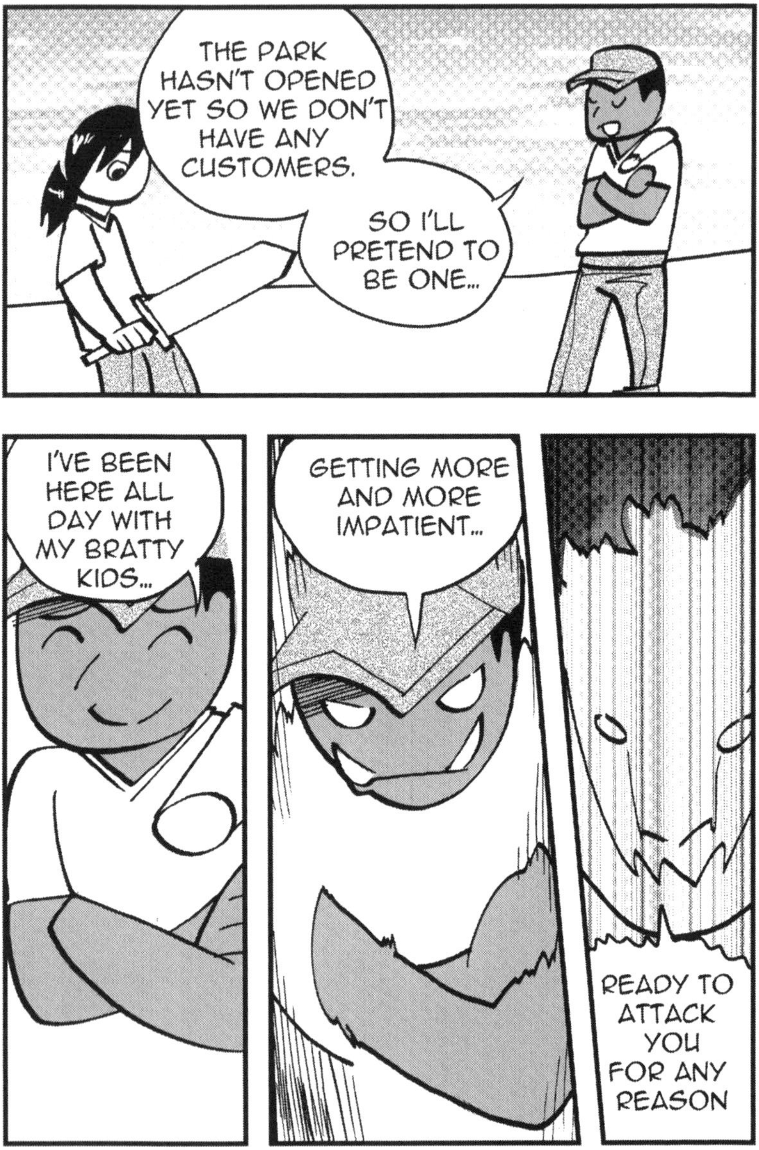
THE PARK HASN'T OPENED YET SO WE DON'T HAVE ANY CUSTOMERS.
SO I'LL PRETEND TO BE ONE...
I'VE BEEN HERE ALL DAY WITH MY BRATTY KIDS...
GETTING MORE AND MORE IMPATIENT...
READY TO ATTACK YOU FOR ANY REASON

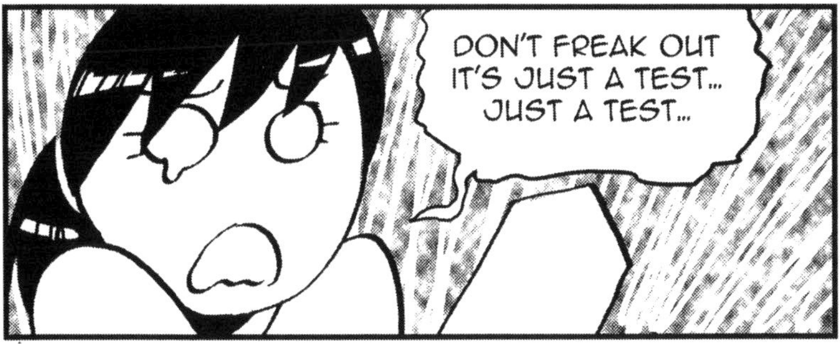
DON'T FREAK OUT
IT'S JUST A TEST...
JUST A TEST...

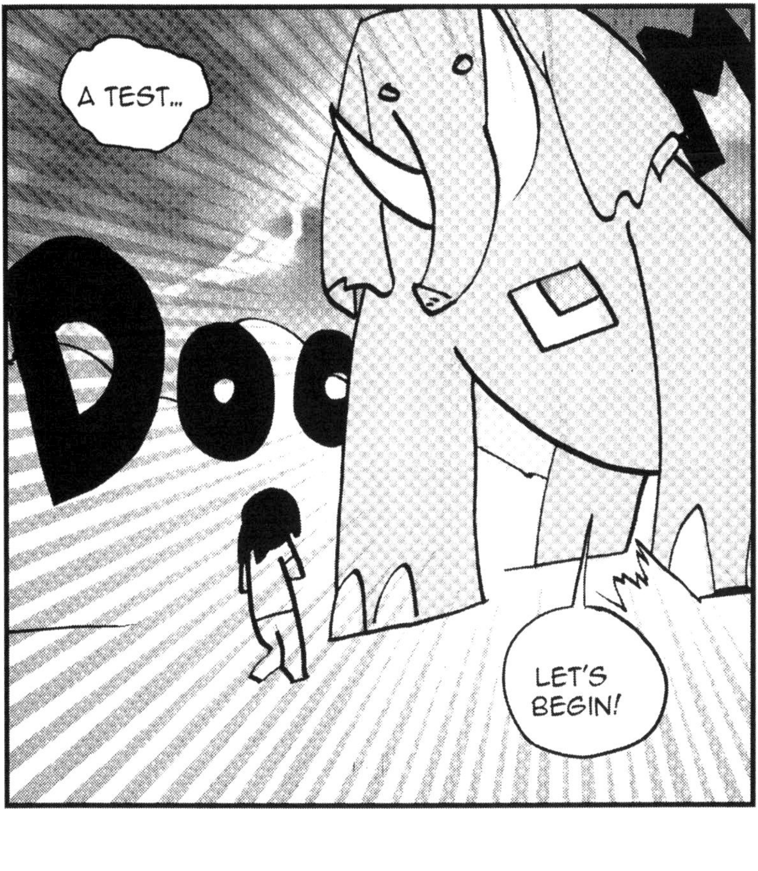
A TEST...
DOO
LET'S
BEGIN!

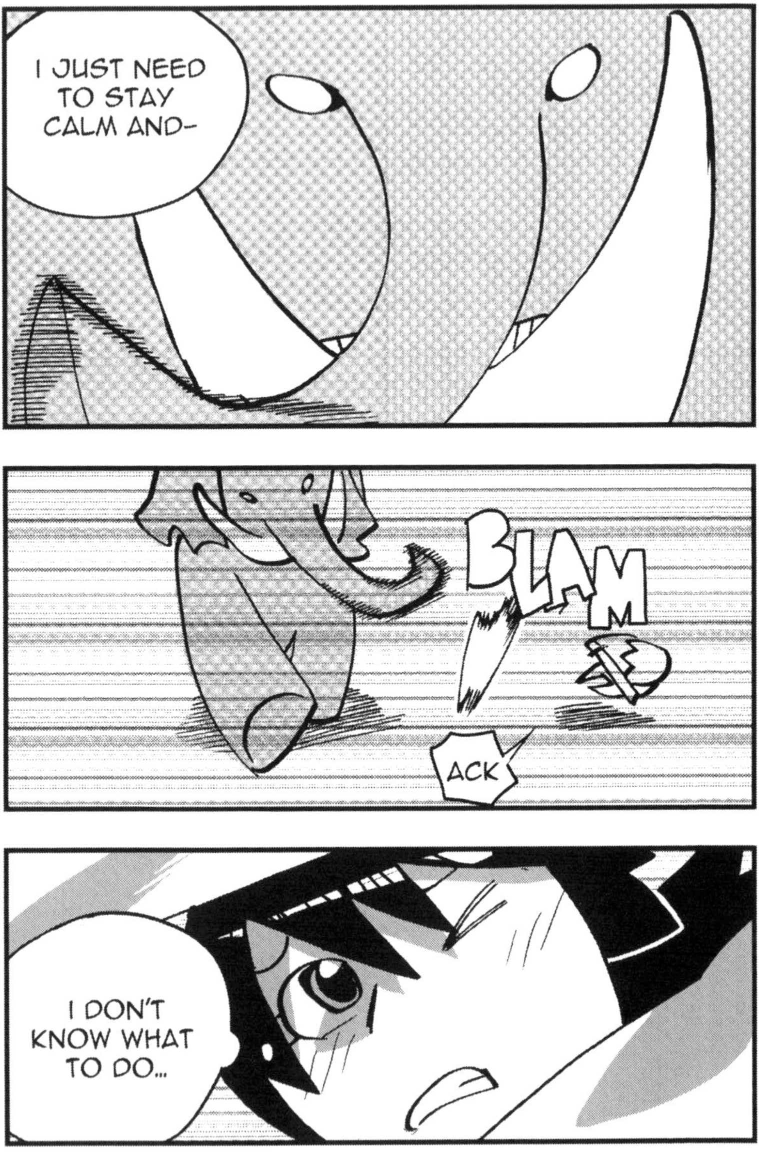
I JUST NEED TO STAY CALM AND-
BLAM
ACK
I DON'T KNOW WHAT TO DO...

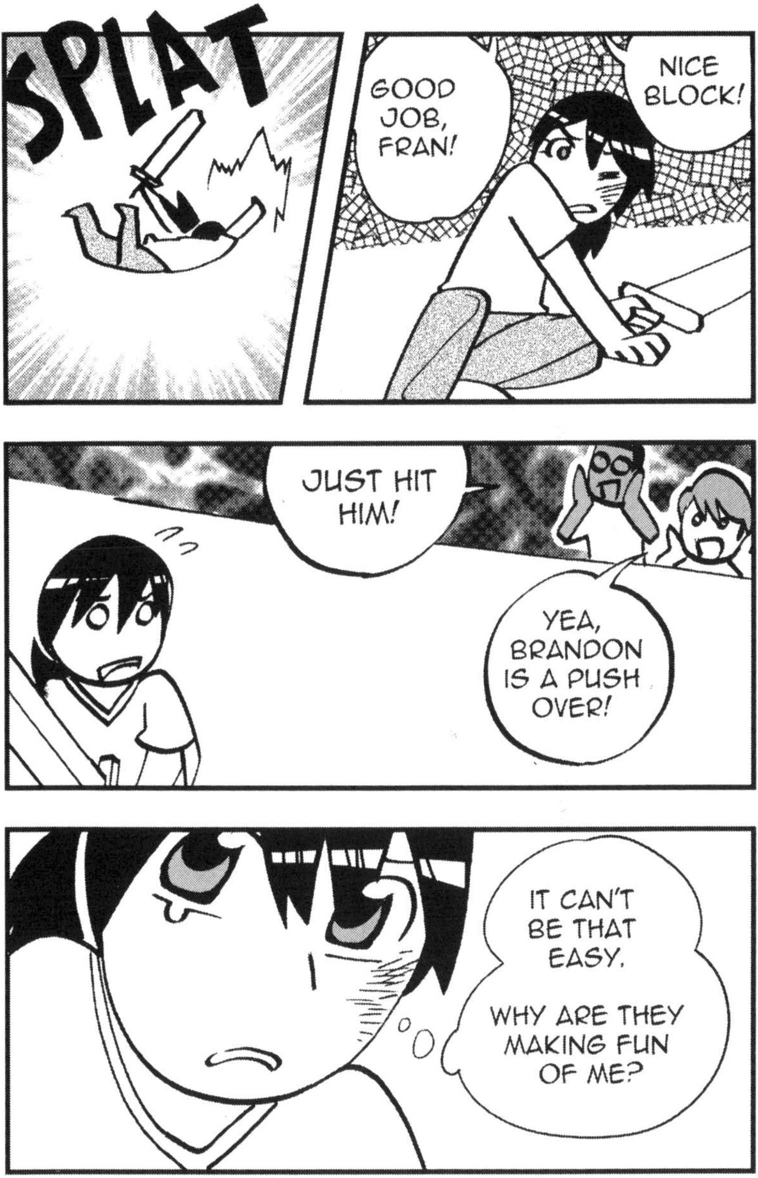
SPLAT
GOOD JOB, FRAN!
NICE BLOCK!
JUST HIT HIM!
YEA, BRANDON IS A PUSH OVER!
IT CAN'T BE THAT EASY.
WHY ARE THEY MAKING FUN OF ME?

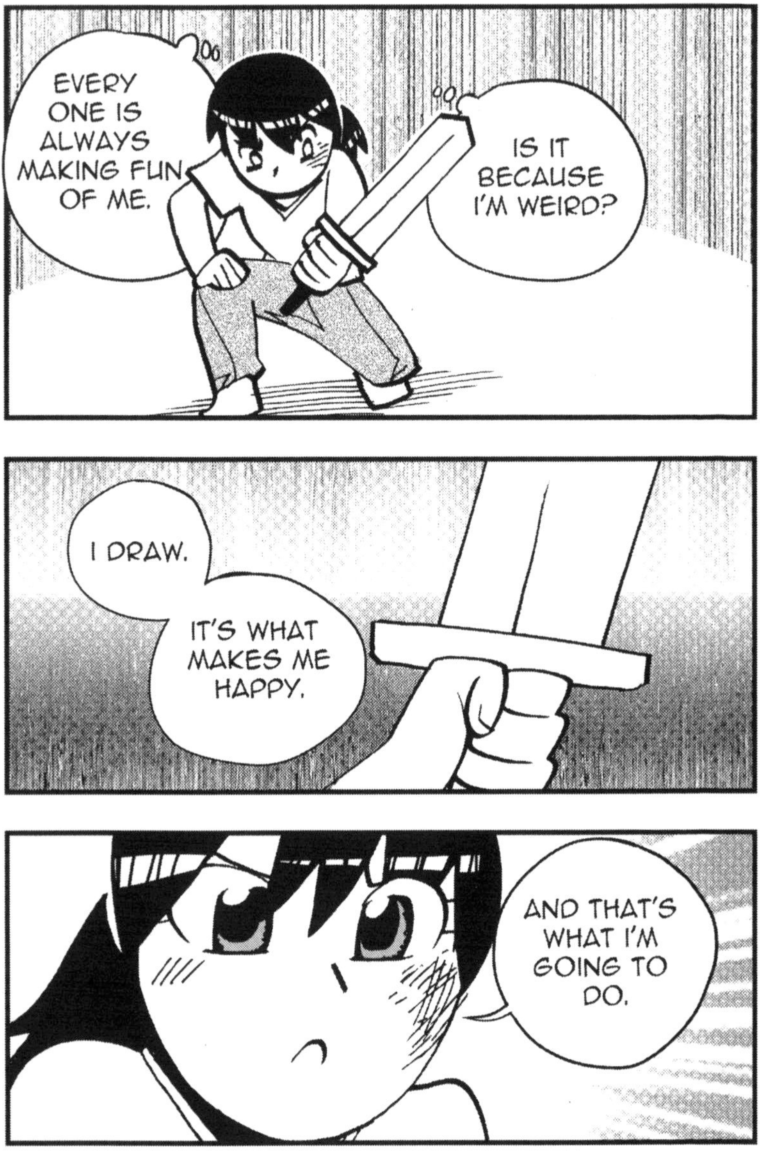
EVERY ONE IS ALWAYS MAKING FUN OF ME.
IS IT BECAUSE I'M WEIRD?
I DRAW.
IT'S WHAT MAKES ME HAPPY.
AND THAT'S WHAT I'M GOING TO DO.

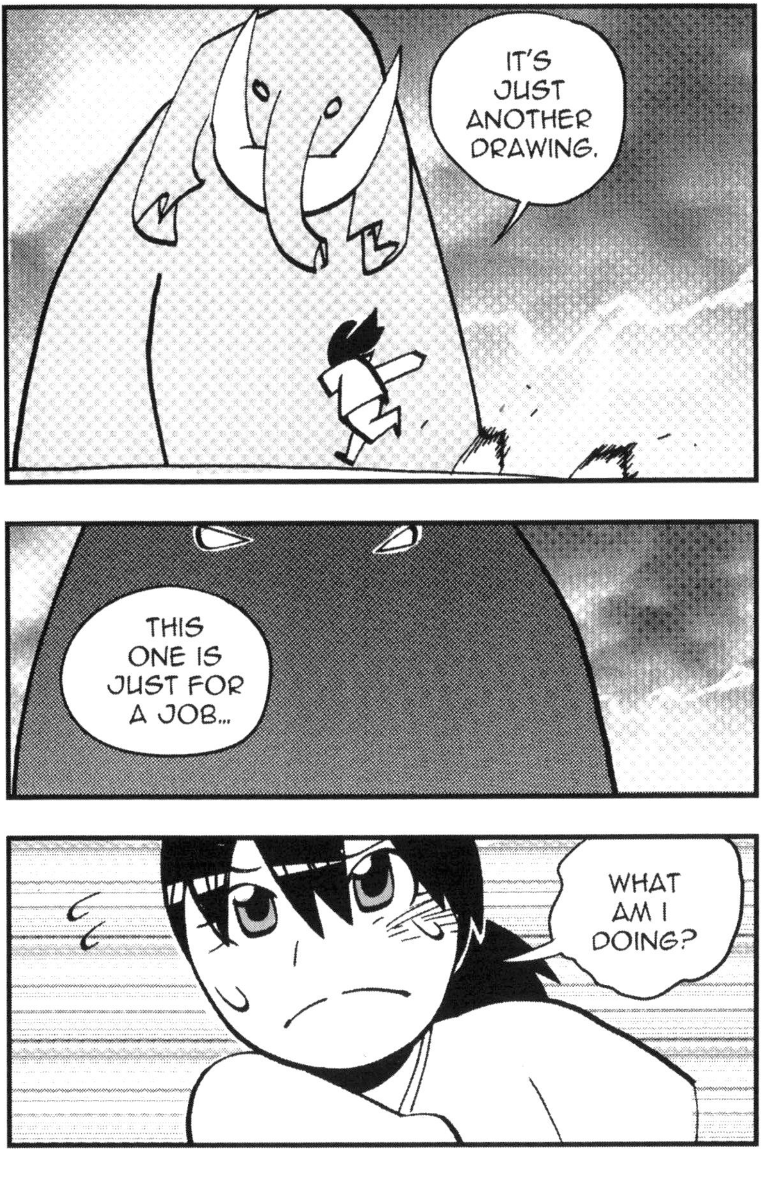
IT'S JUST ANOTHER DRAWING.
THIS ONE IS JUST FOR A JOB...
WHAT AM I DOING?

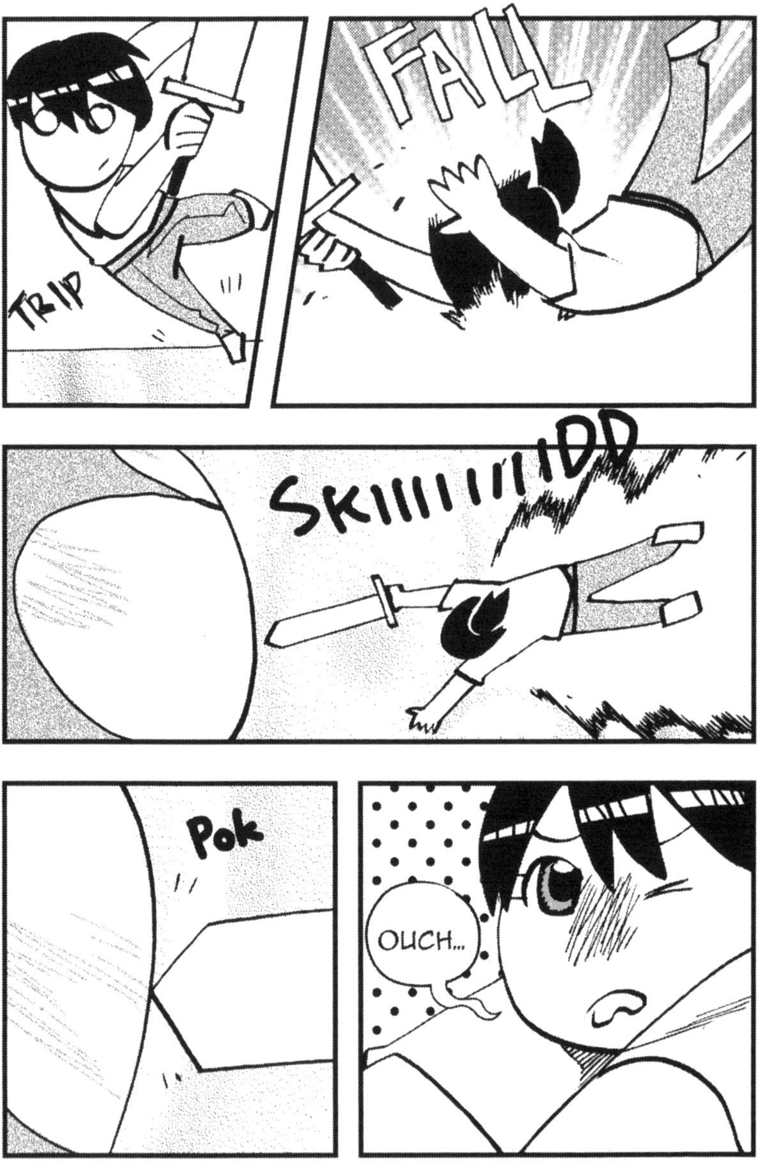
TRIP
FALL
SKIIIIIIIIDD
Pok
OUCH...

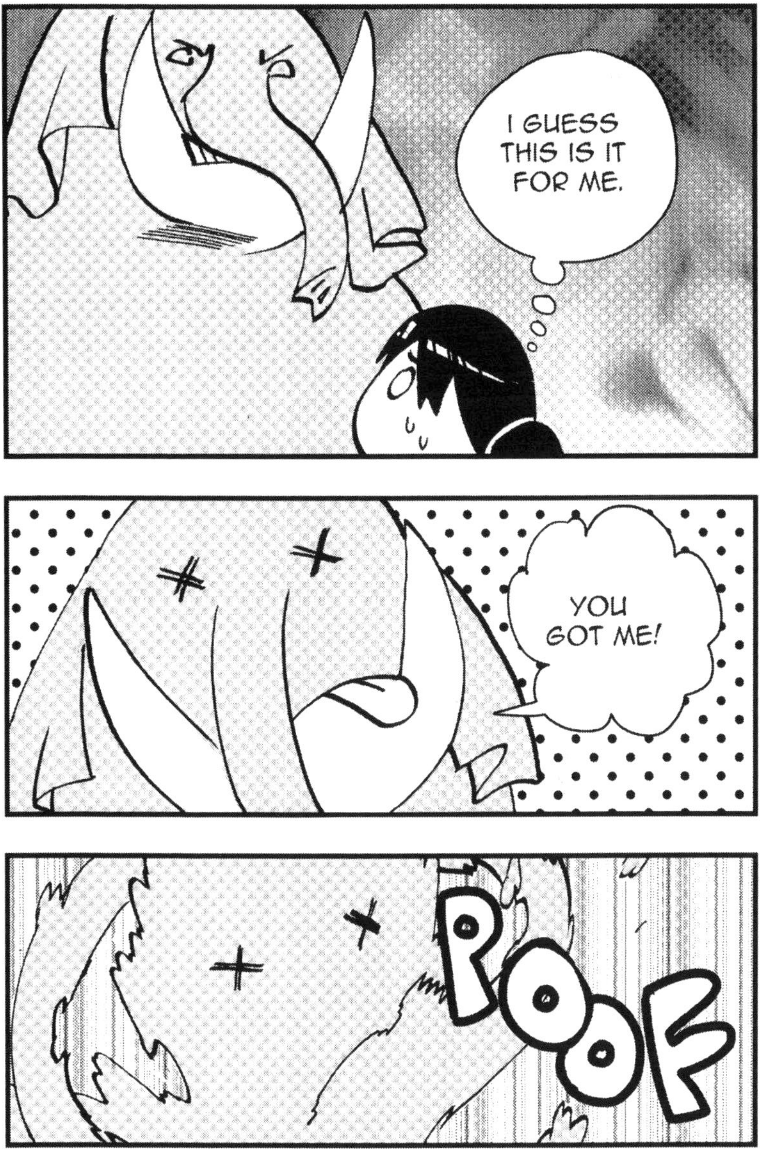
I GUESS THIS IS IT FOR ME.
YOU GOT ME!
POOF

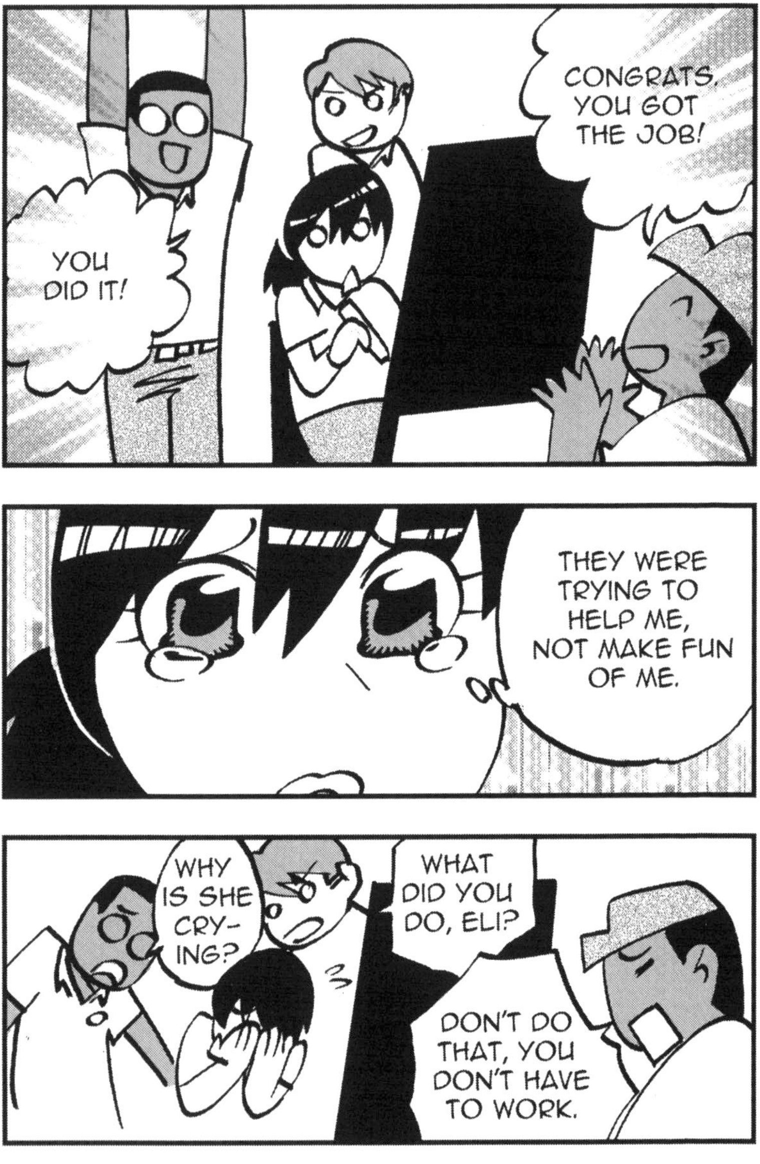

YOU DID IT!
CONGRATS. YOU GOT THE JOB!
THEY WERE TRYING TO HELP ME, NOT MAKE FUN OF ME.
WHY IS SHE CRY-ING?
WHAT DID YOU DO, ELI?
DON'T DO THAT, YOU DON'T HAVE TO WORK.

Art Lesson 4

DRAWING IS THE HONESTY OF THE ART. THERE IS NO
POSSIBILITY OF CHEATING. IT IS EITHER GOOD OR BAD.
-SALVADOR DALI

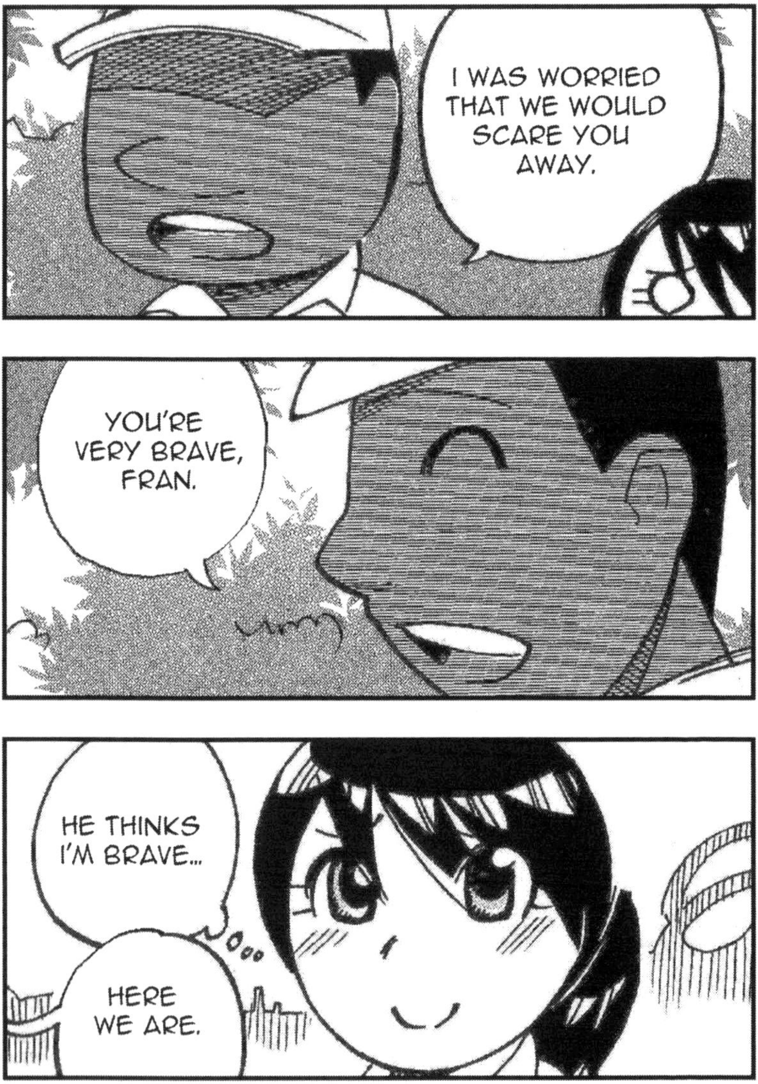
I WAS WORRIED THAT WE WOULD SCARE YOU AWAY.
YOU'RE VERY BRAVE, FRAN.
HE THINKS I'M BRAVE...
HERE WE ARE.

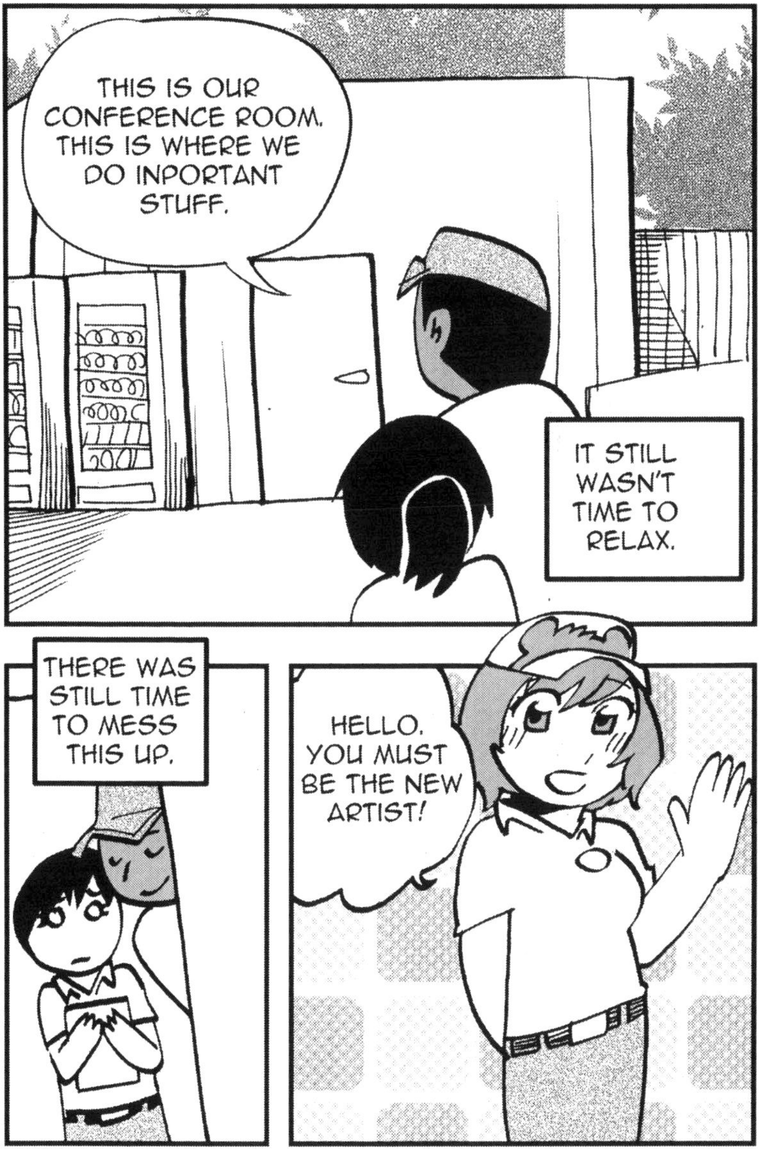
THIS IS OUR CONFERENCE ROOM. THIS IS WHERE WE DO INPORTANT STUFF.
IT STILL WASN'T TIME TO RELAX.
THERE WAS STILL TIME TO MESS THIS UP.
HELLO. YOU MUST BE THE NEW ARTIST!

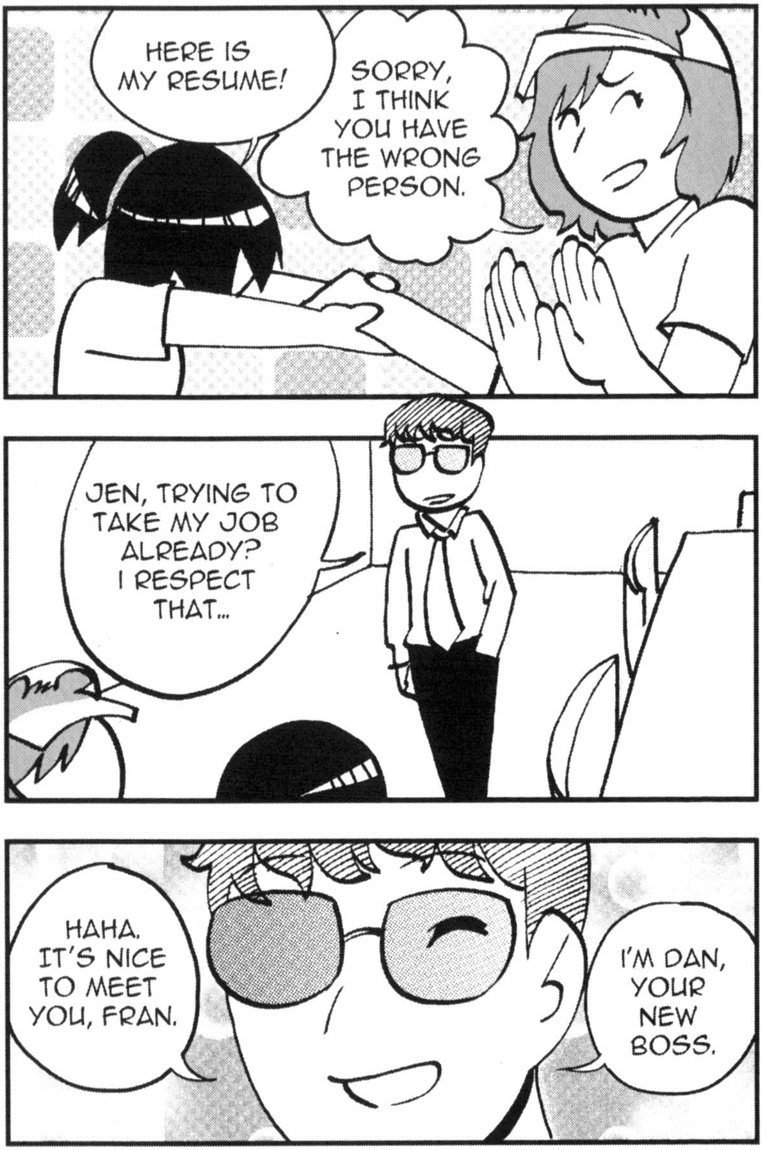
HERE IS MY RESUME!
SORRY, I THINK YOU HAVE THE WRONG PERSON.
JEN, TRYING TO TAKE MY JOB ALREADY? I RESPECT THAT...
HAHA. IT'S NICE TO MEET YOU, FRAN.
I'M DAN, YOUR NEW BOSS.

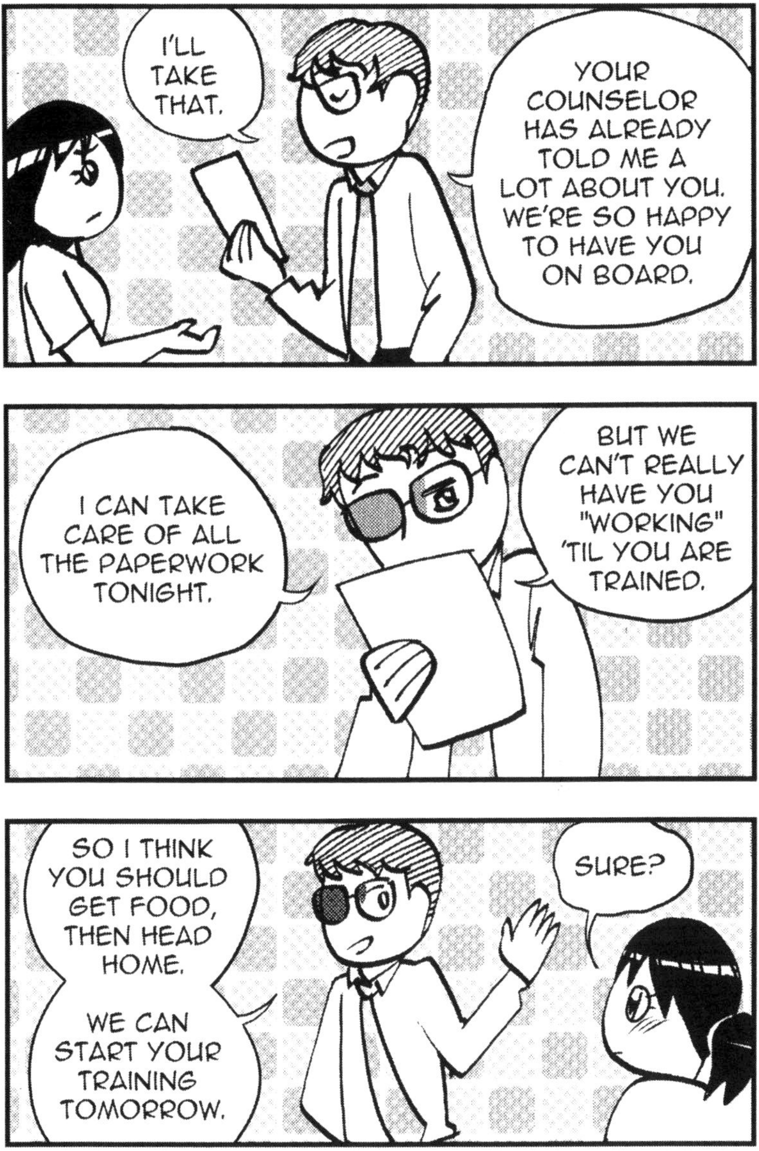
I'LL TAKE THAT.
YOUR COUNSELOR HAS ALREADY TOLD ME A LOT ABOUT YOU. WE'RE SO HAPPY TO HAVE YOU ON BOARD.
I CAN TAKE CARE OF ALL THE PAPERWORK TONIGHT.
BUT WE CAN'T REALLY HAVE YOU "WORKING" 'TIL YOU ARE TRAINED.
SO I THINK YOU SHOULD GET FOOD, THEN HEAD HOME.
WE CAN START YOUR TRAINING TOMORROW.
SURE?

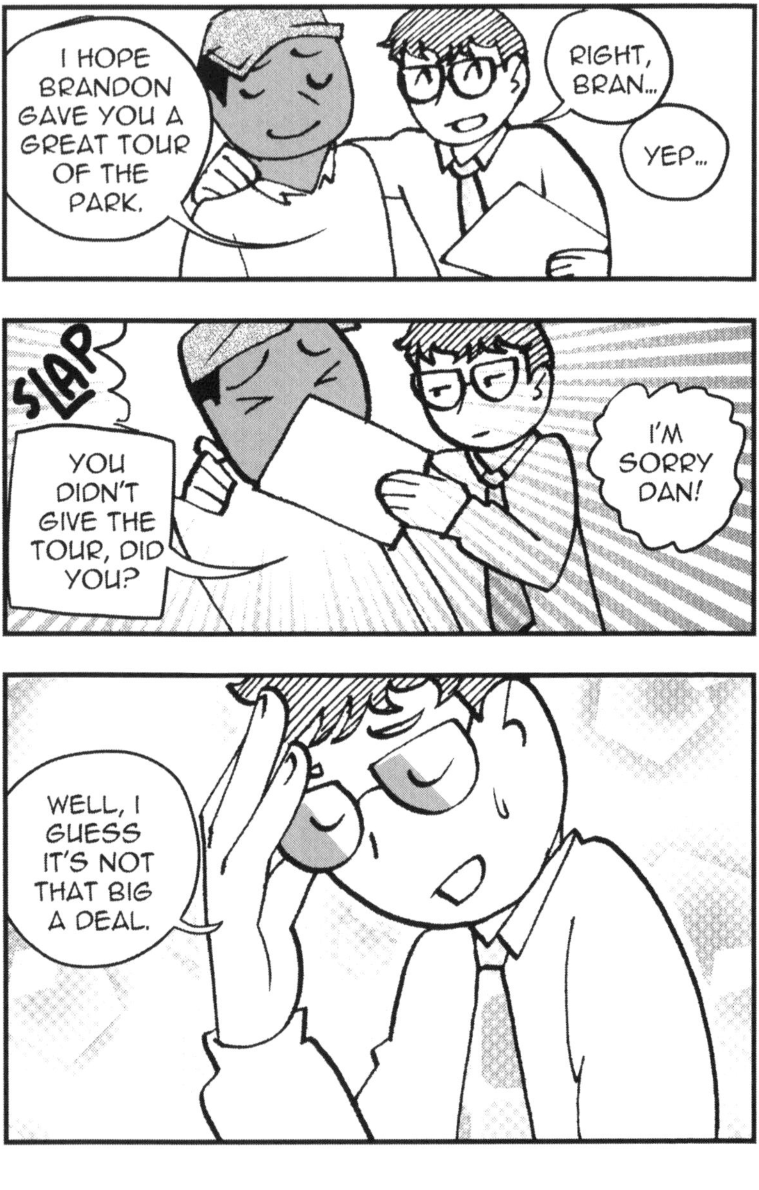
I HOPE BRANDON GAVE YOU A GREAT TOUR OF THE PARK.
RIGHT, BRAN...
YEP...
SLAP
YOU DIDN'T GIVE THE TOUR, DID YOU?
I'M SORRY DAN!
WELL, I GUESS IT'S NOT THAT BIG A DEAL.

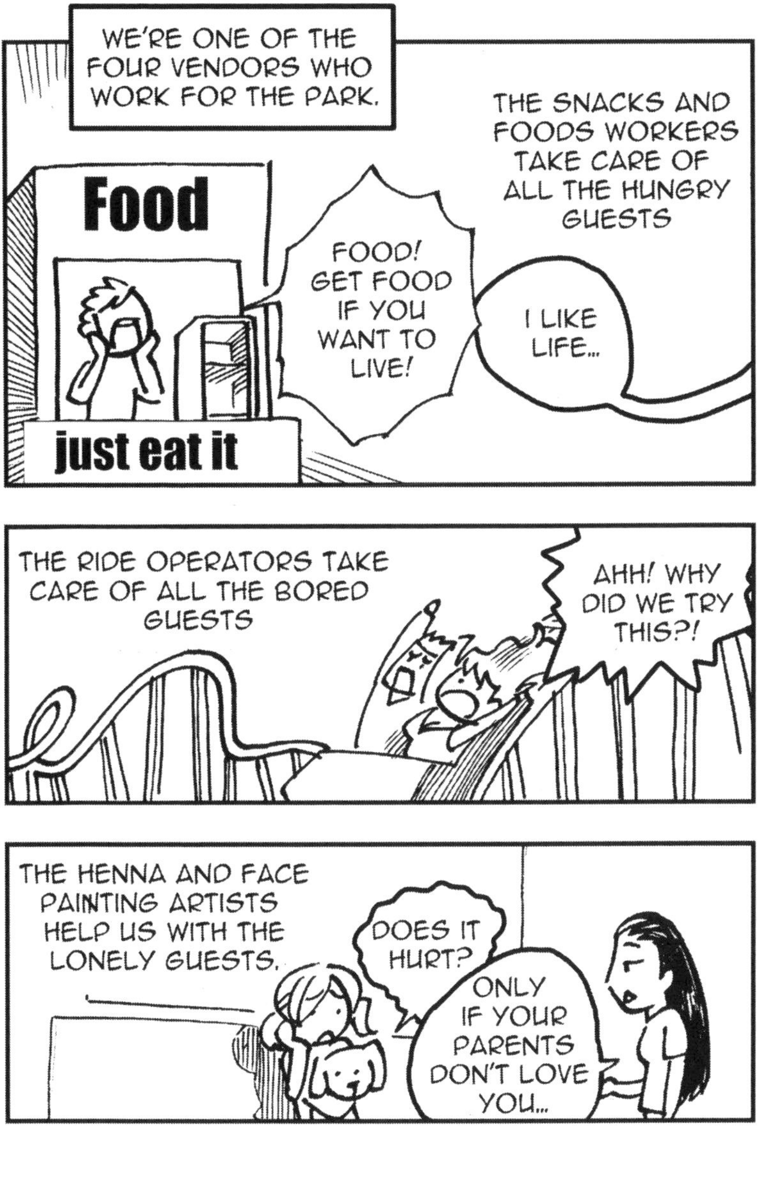
WE'RE ONE OF THE FOUR VENDORS WHO WORK FOR THE PARK.
THE SNACKS AND FOODS WORKERS TAKE CARE OF ALL THE HUNGRY GUESTS
Food
just eat it
FOOD! GET FOOD IF YOU WANT TO LIVE!
I LIKE LIFE...
THE RIDE OPERATORS TAKE CARE OF ALL THE BORED GUESTS
AHH! WHY DID WE TRY THIS?!
THE HENNA AND FACE PAINTING ARTISTS HELP US WITH THE LONELY GUESTS.
DOES IT HURT?
ONLY IF YOUR PARENTS DON'T LOVE YOU...

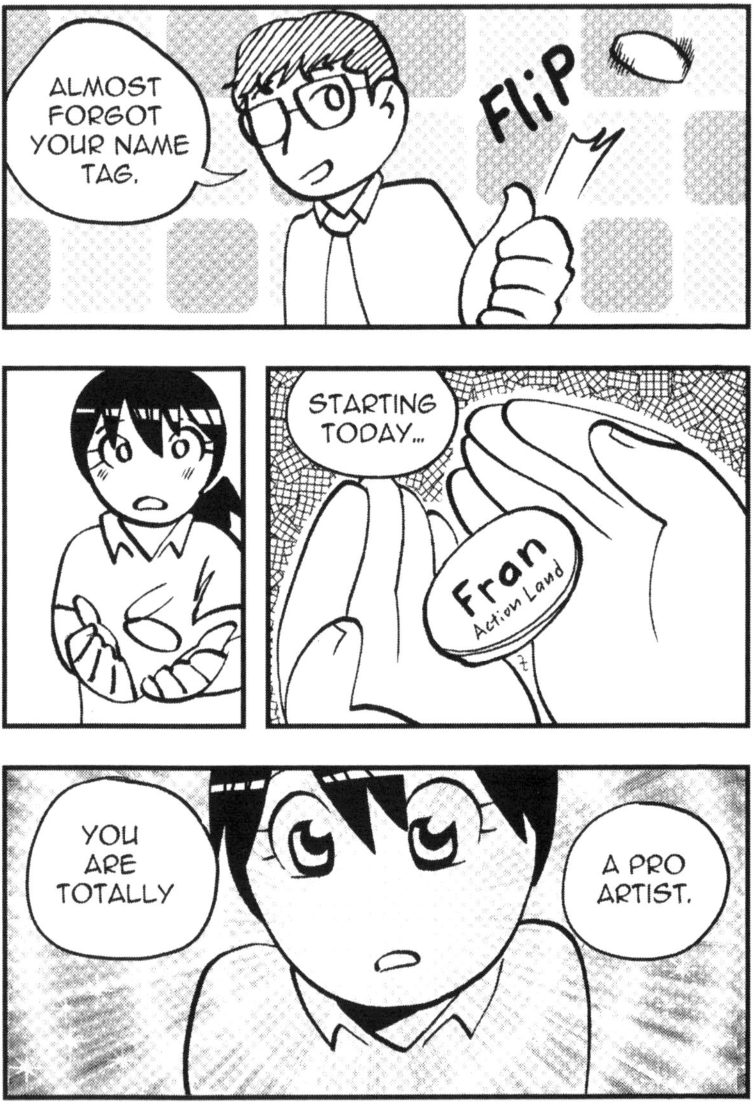
ALMOST FORGOT YOUR NAME TAG.
FliP
STARTING TODAY...
Fran
Action Land
YOU ARE TOTALLY
A PRO ARTIST.

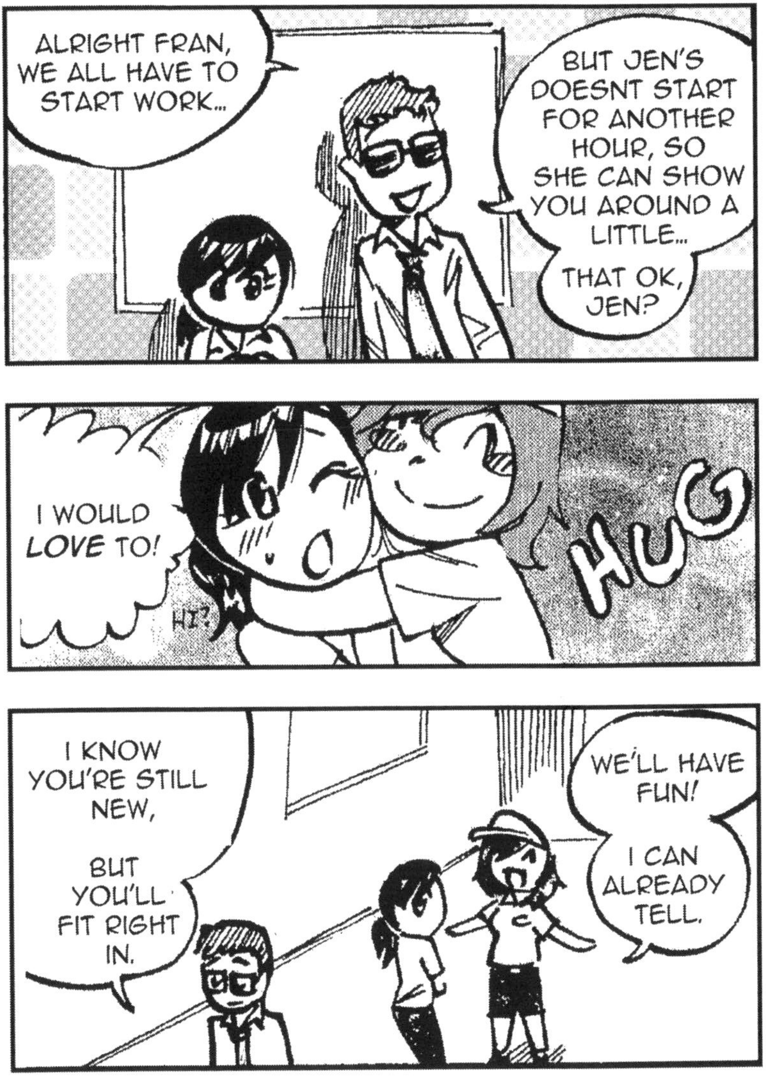
ALRIGHT FRAN, WE ALL HAVE TO START WORK...
BUT JEN'S DOESNT START FOR ANOTHER HOUR, SO SHE CAN SHOW YOU AROUND A LITTLE...
THAT OK, JEN?
I WOULD *LOVE* TO!
HI?
HUG
I KNOW YOU'RE STILL NEW,
BUT YOU'LL FIT RIGHT IN.
WE'LL HAVE FUN!
I CAN ALREADY TELL.

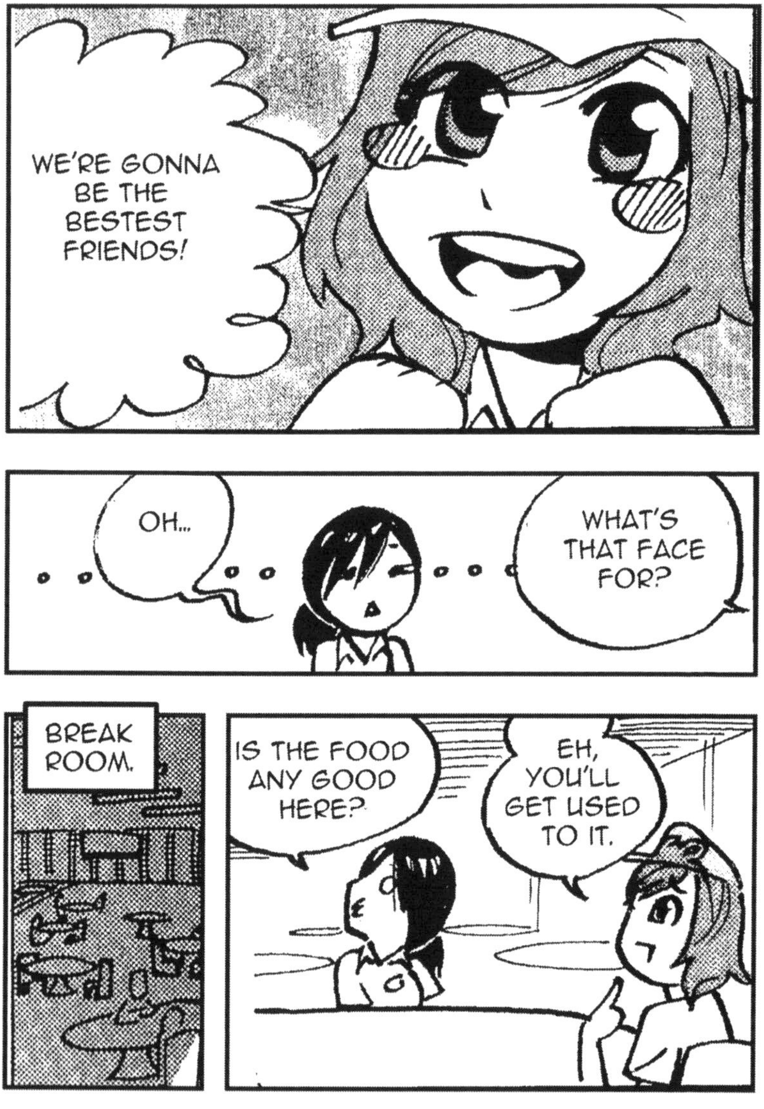
WE'RE GONNA BE THE BESTEST FRIENDS!
OH...
WHAT'S THAT FACE FOR?
BREAK ROOM.
IS THE FOOD ANY GOOD HERE?
EH, YOU'LL GET USED TO IT.

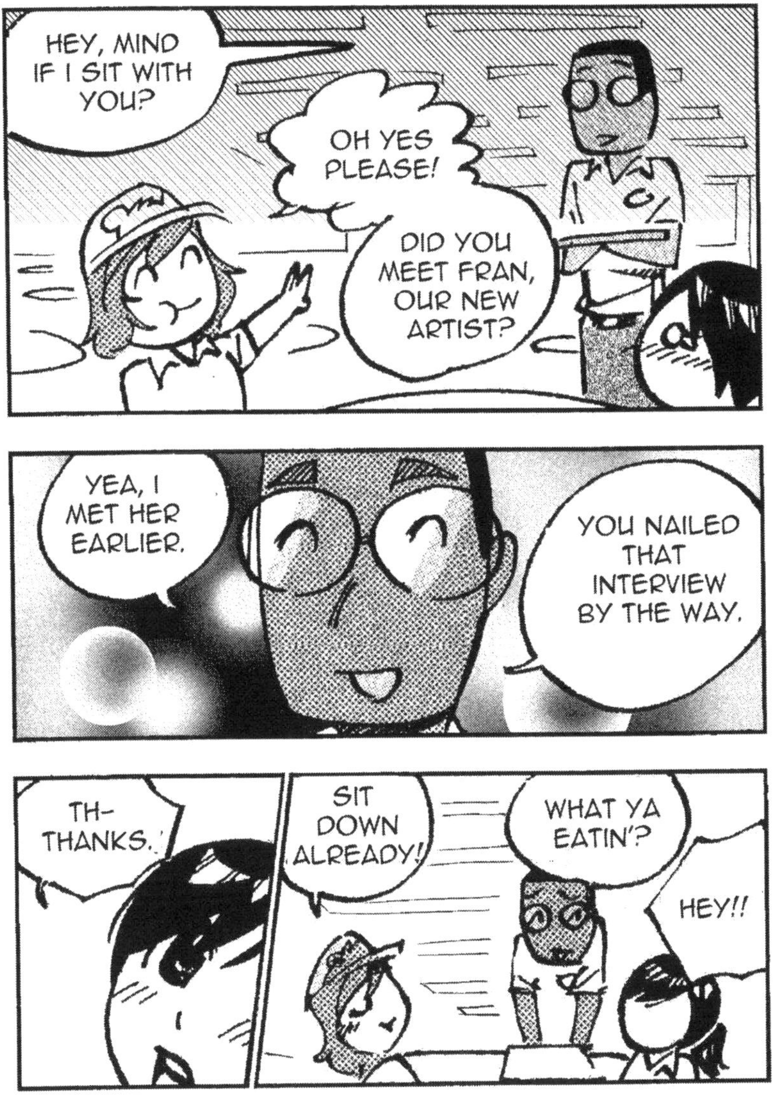
HEY, MIND IF I SIT WITH YOU?
OH YES PLEASE!
DID YOU MEET FRAN, OUR NEW ARTIST?
YEA, I MET HER EARLIER.
YOU NAILED THAT INTERVIEW BY THE WAY.
TH- THANKS.
SIT DOWN ALREADY!
WHAT YA EATIN'?
HEY!!

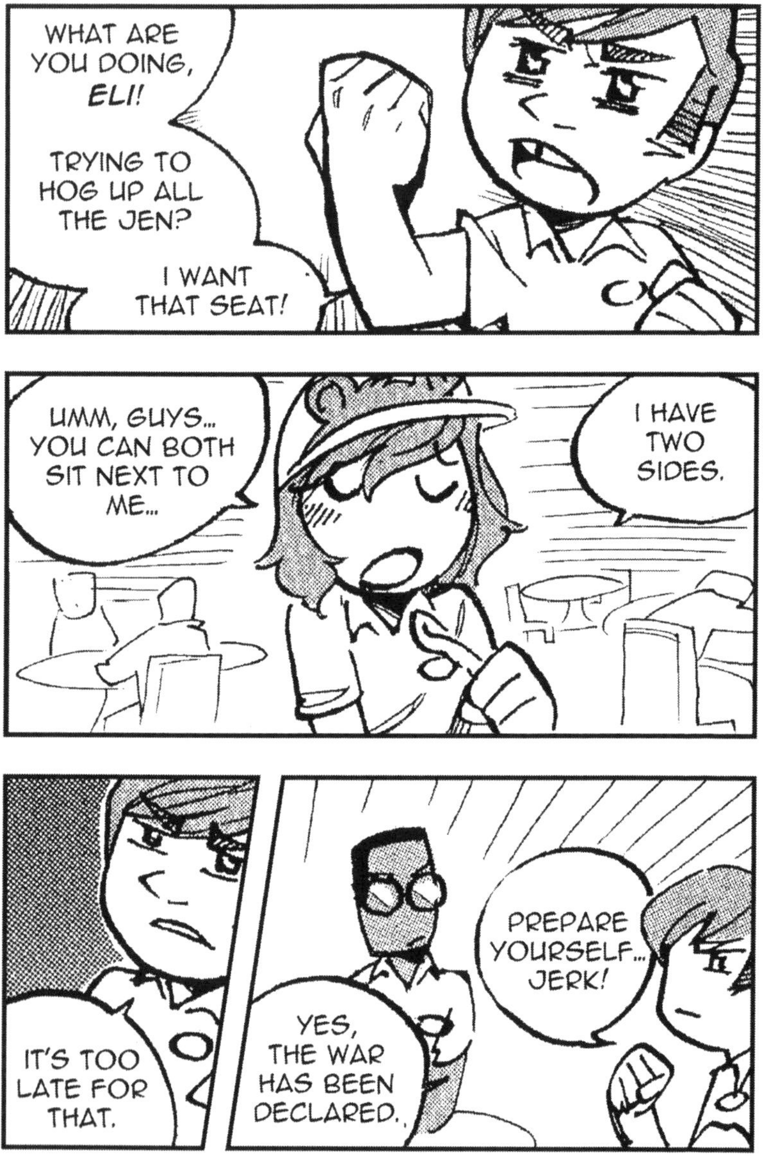
WHAT ARE YOU DOING, ELI!
TRYING TO HOG UP ALL THE JEN?
I WANT THAT SEAT!
UMM, GUYS... YOU CAN BOTH SIT NEXT TO ME...
I HAVE TWO SIDES.
IT'S TOO LATE FOR THAT.
PREPARE YOURSELF... JERK!
YES, THE WAR HAS BEEN DECLARED.

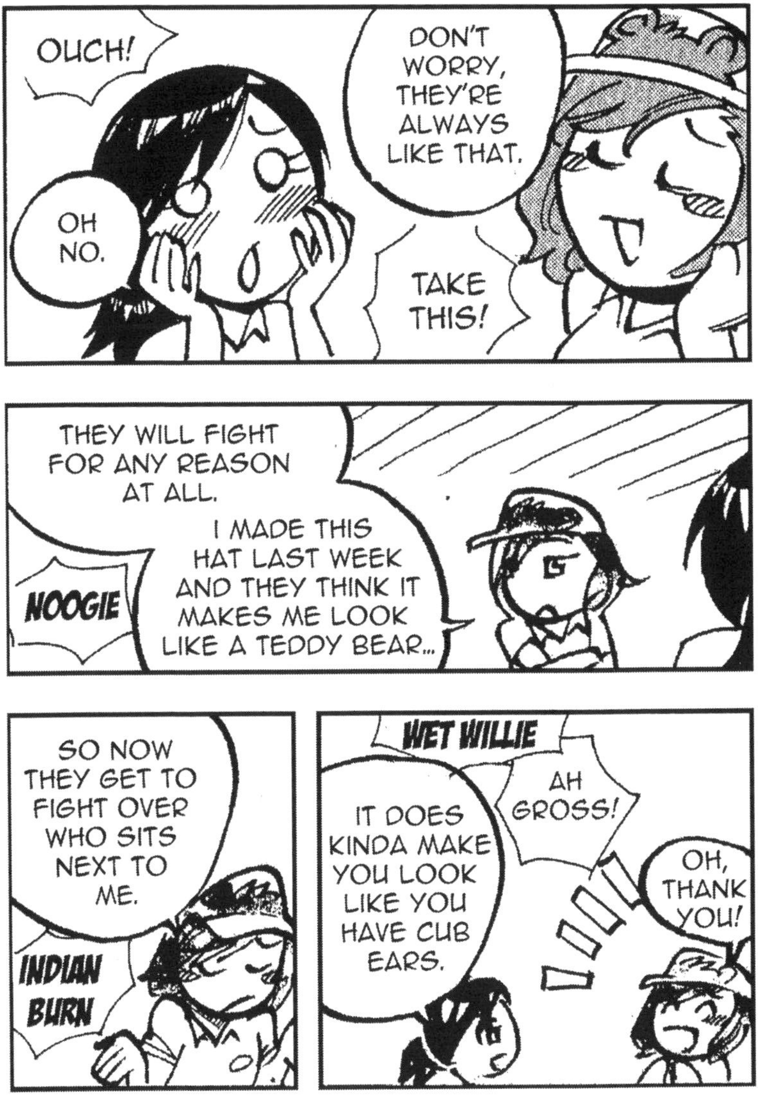
OUCH!
OH NO.
DON'T WORRY, THEY'RE ALWAYS LIKE THAT.
TAKE THIS!
THEY WILL FIGHT FOR ANY REASON AT ALL.
NOOGIE
I MADE THIS HAT LAST WEEK AND THEY THINK IT MAKES ME LOOK LIKE A TEDDY BEAR...
SO NOW THEY GET TO FIGHT OVER WHO SITS NEXT TO ME.
INDIAN BURN
WET WILLIE
IT DOES KINDA MAKE YOU LOOK LIKE YOU HAVE CUB EARS.
AH GROSS!
OH, THANK YOU!

Art Lesson 5

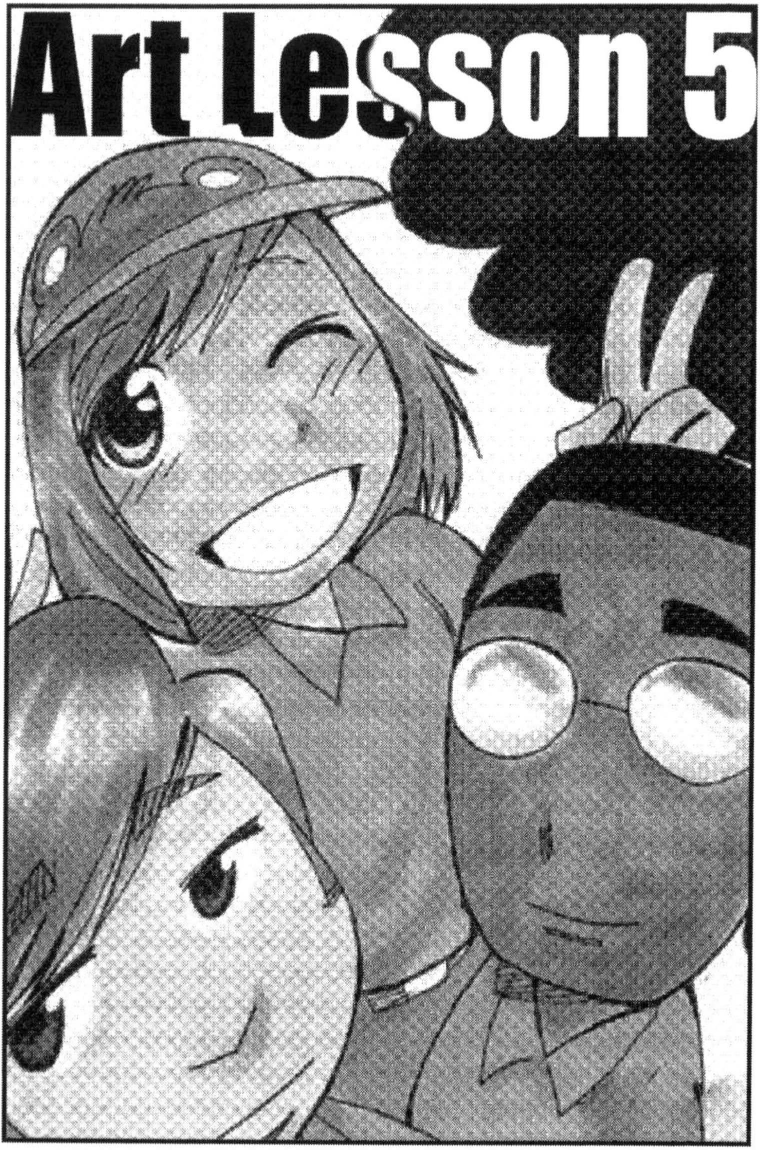

VISION IS THE ART OF SEEING WHAT IS INVISIBLE TO OTHERS.
-JONATHAN SWIFT

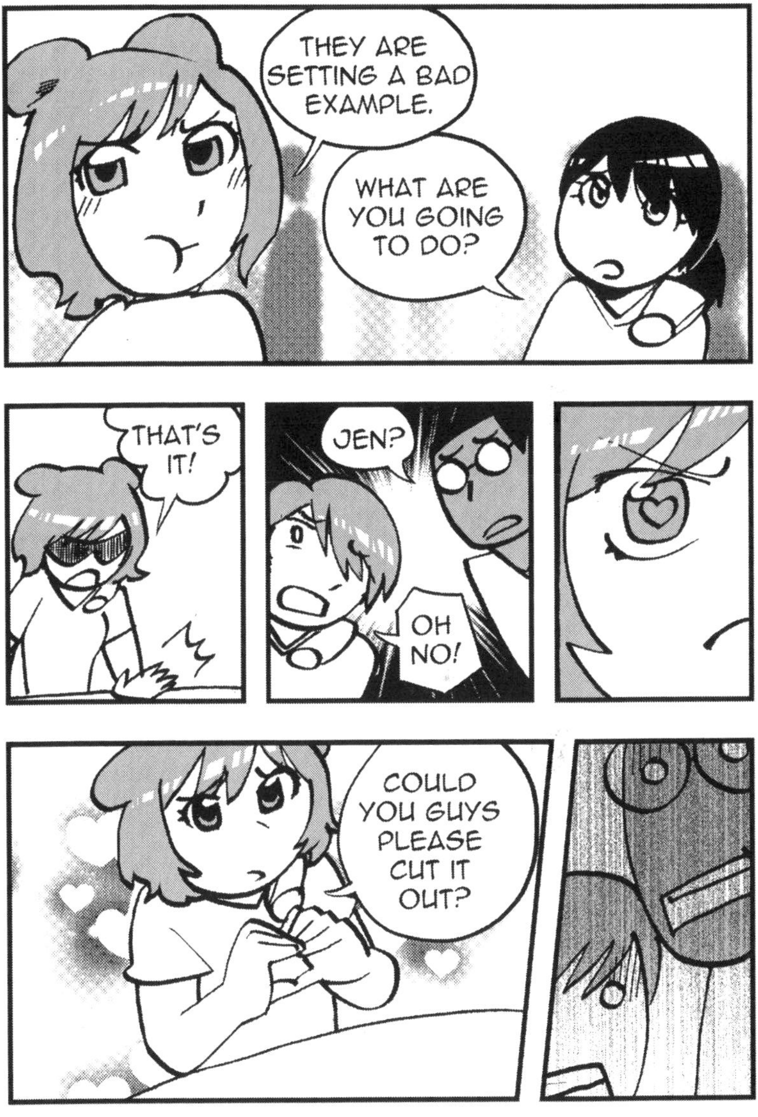
THEY ARE SETTING A BAD EXAMPLE.
WHAT ARE YOU GOING TO DO?
THAT'S IT!
JEN?
OH NO!
COULD YOU GUYS PLEASE CUT IT OUT?

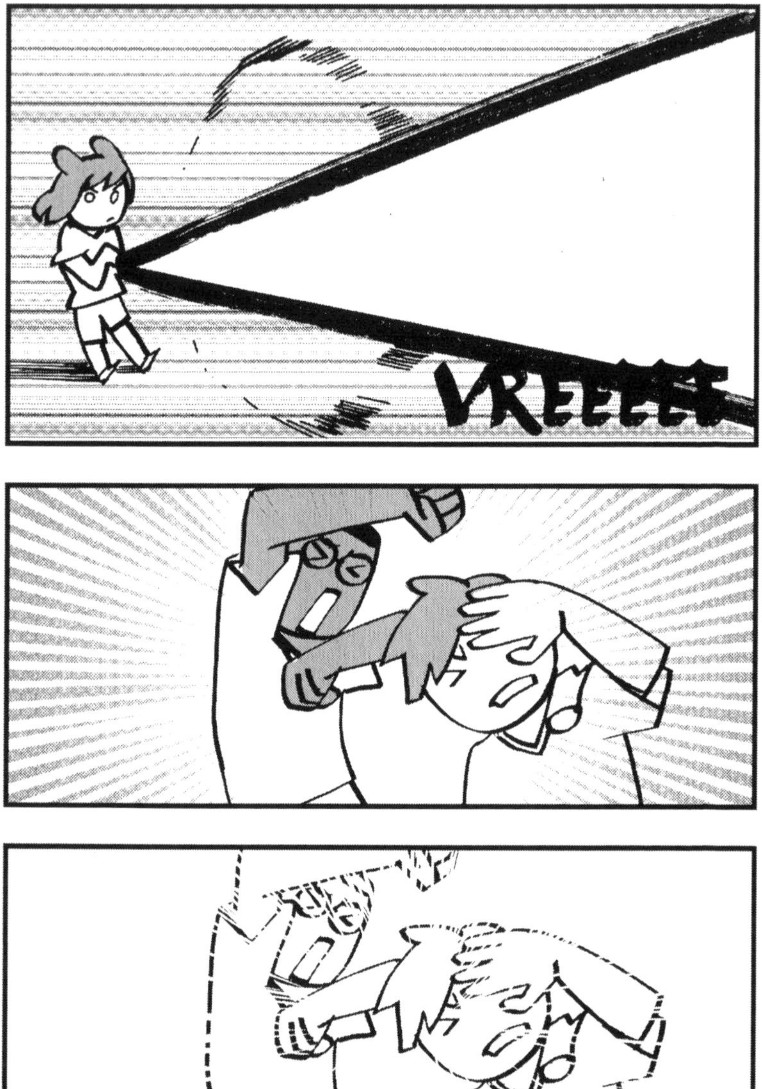
VREEEEE

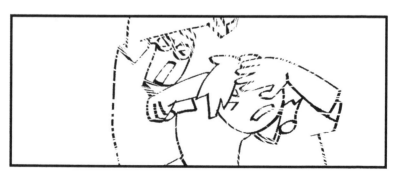

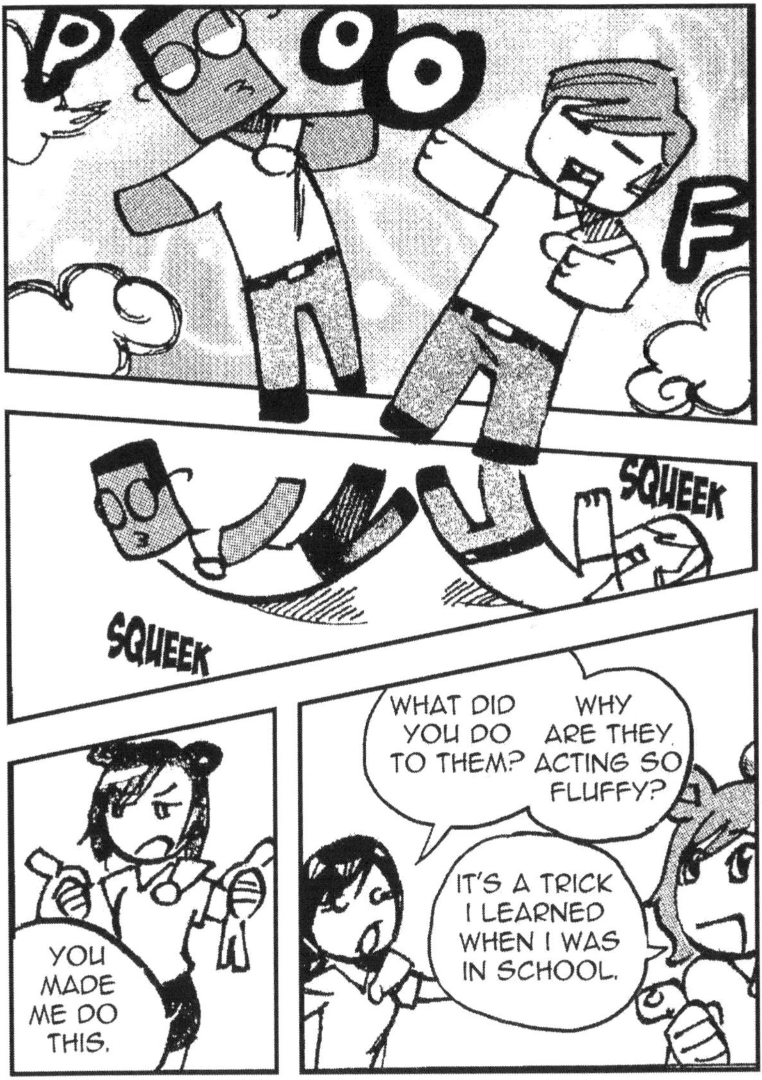
POOF
SQUEEK
SQUEEK
YOU MADE ME DO THIS.
WHAT DID YOU DO TO THEM?
WHY ARE THEY ACTING SO FLUFFY?
IT'S A TRICK I LEARNED WHEN I WAS IN SCHOOL.

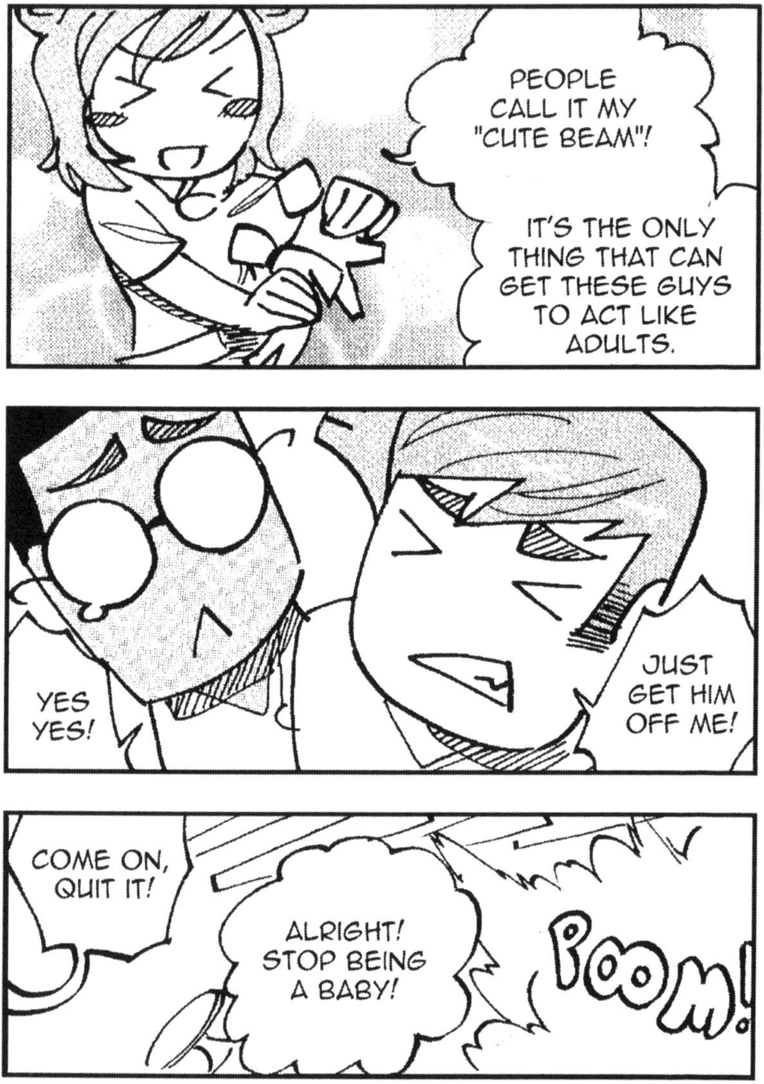
PEOPLE CALL IT MY "CUTE BEAM"!
IT'S THE ONLY THING THAT CAN GET THESE GUYS TO ACT LIKE ADULTS.
YES YES!
JUST GET HIM OFF ME!
COME ON, QUIT IT!
ALRIGHT! STOP BEING A BABY!
POOM!

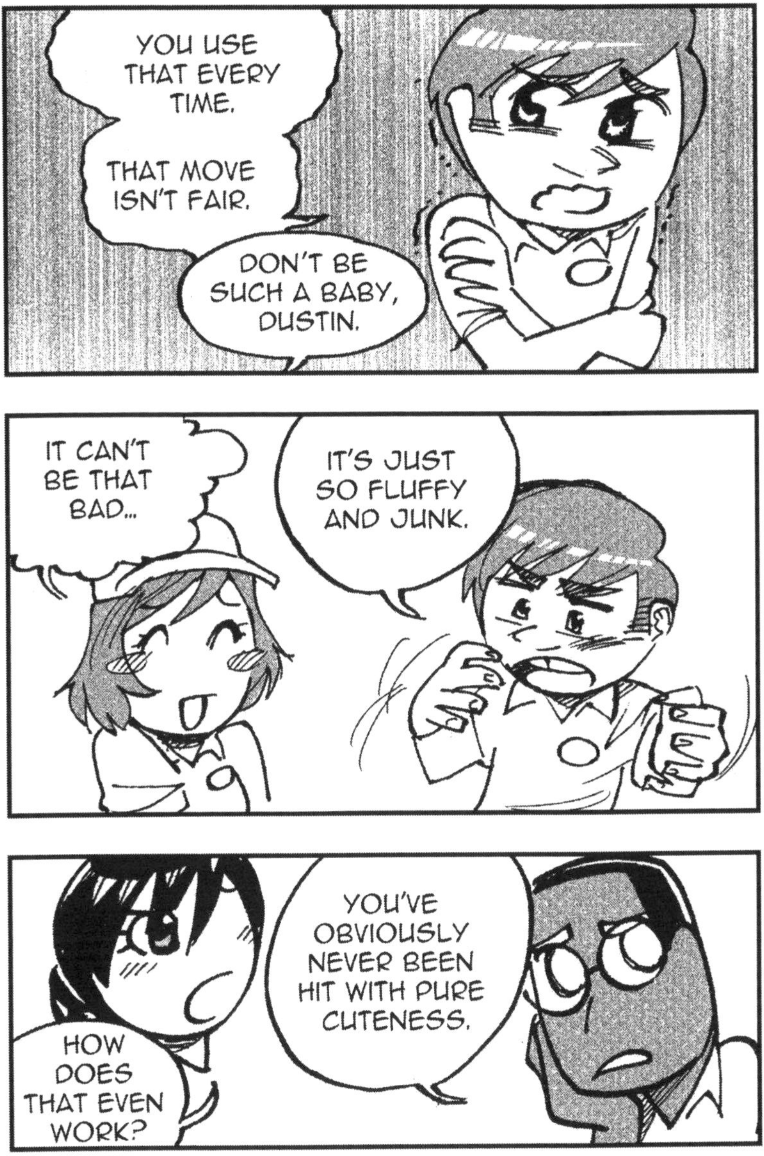
YOU USE THAT EVERY TIME.
THAT MOVE ISN'T FAIR.
DON'T BE SUCH A BABY, DUSTIN.
IT CAN'T BE THAT BAD...
IT'S JUST SO FLUFFY AND JUNK.
YOU'VE OBVIOUSLY NEVER BEEN HIT WITH PURE CUTENESS.
HOW DOES THAT EVEN WORK?

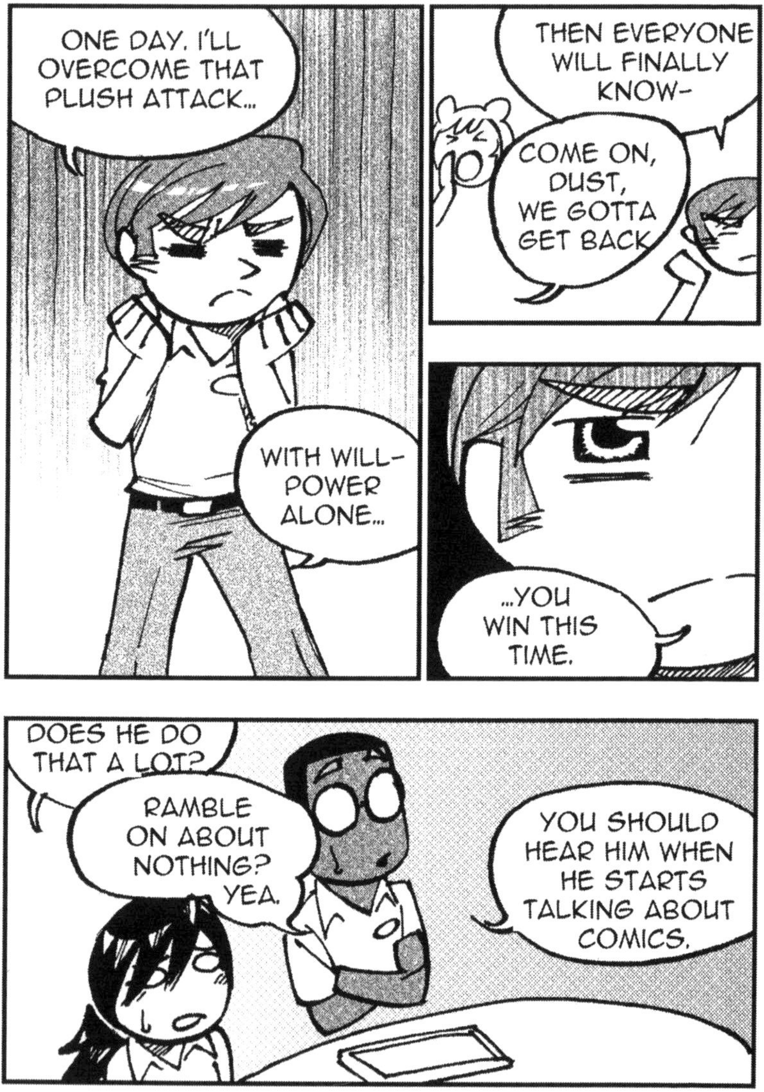
ONE DAY, I'LL OVERCOME THAT PLUSH ATTACK...
WITH WILL-POWER ALONE...
THEN EVERYONE WILL FINALLY KNOW-
COME ON, DUST, WE GOTTA GET BACK
...YOU WIN THIS TIME.
DOES HE DO THAT A LOT?
RAMBLE ON ABOUT NOTHING? YEA.
YOU SHOULD HEAR HIM WHEN HE STARTS TALKING ABOUT COMICS.

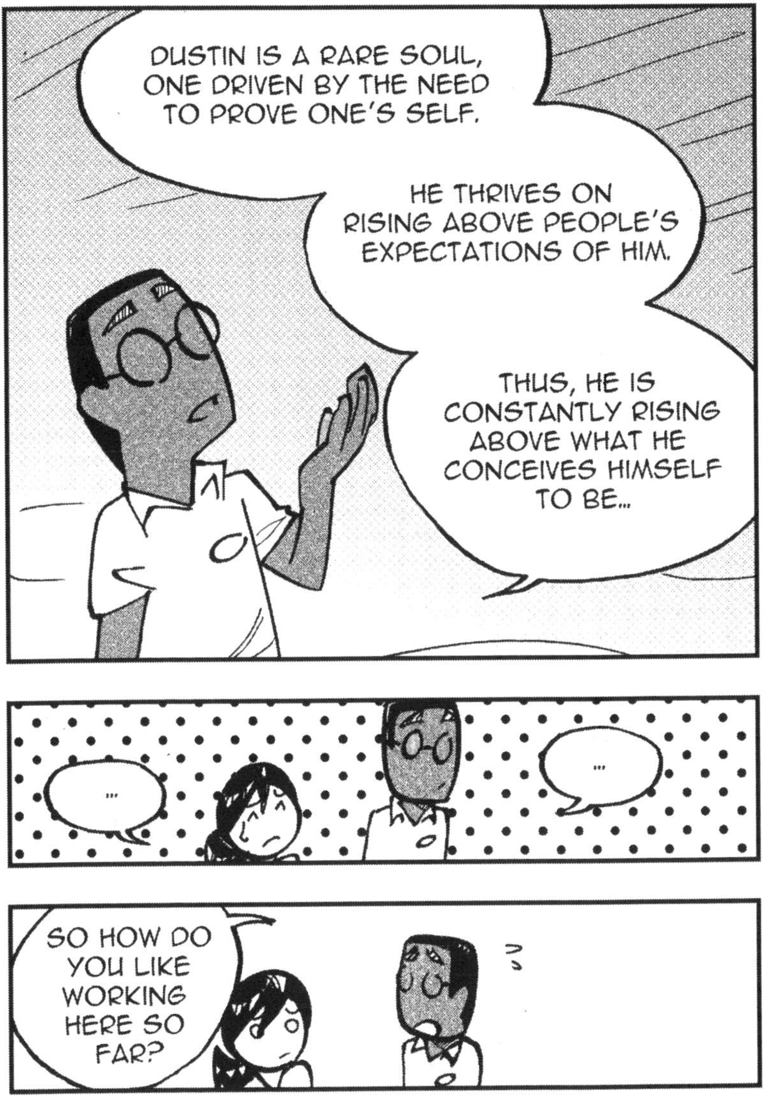
DUSTIN IS A RARE SOUL, ONE DRIVEN BY THE NEED TO PROVE ONE'S SELF.
HE THRIVES ON RISING ABOVE PEOPLE'S EXPECTATIONS OF HIM.
THUS, HE IS CONSTANTLY RISING ABOVE WHAT HE CONCEIVES HIMSELF TO BE...
...
...
SO HOW DO YOU LIKE WORKING HERE SO FAR?

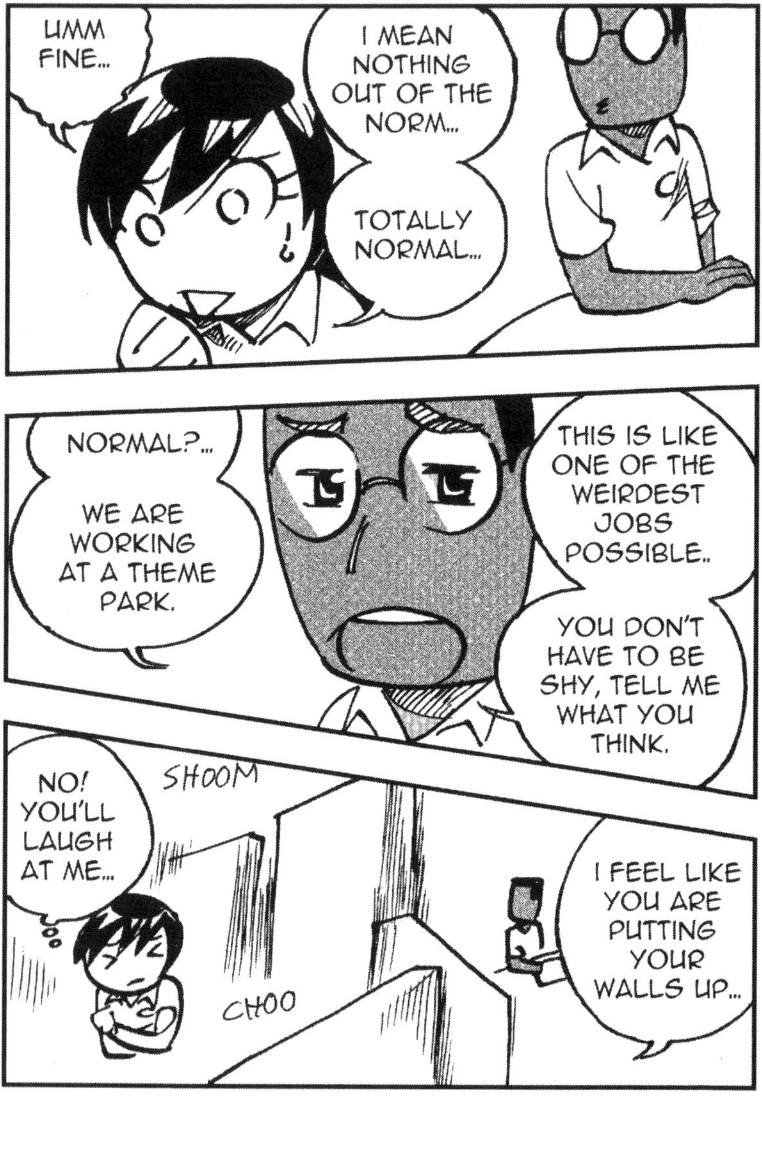
UMM FINE...
I MEAN NOTHING OUT OF THE NORM...
TOTALLY NORMAL...
NORMAL?...
WE ARE WORKING AT A THEME PARK.
THIS IS LIKE ONE OF THE WEIRDEST JOBS POSSIBLE..
YOU DON'T HAVE TO BE SHY, TELL ME WHAT YOU THINK.
NO! YOU'LL LAUGH AT ME...
SHOOM
CHOO
I FEEL LIKE YOU ARE PUTTING YOUR WALLS UP...

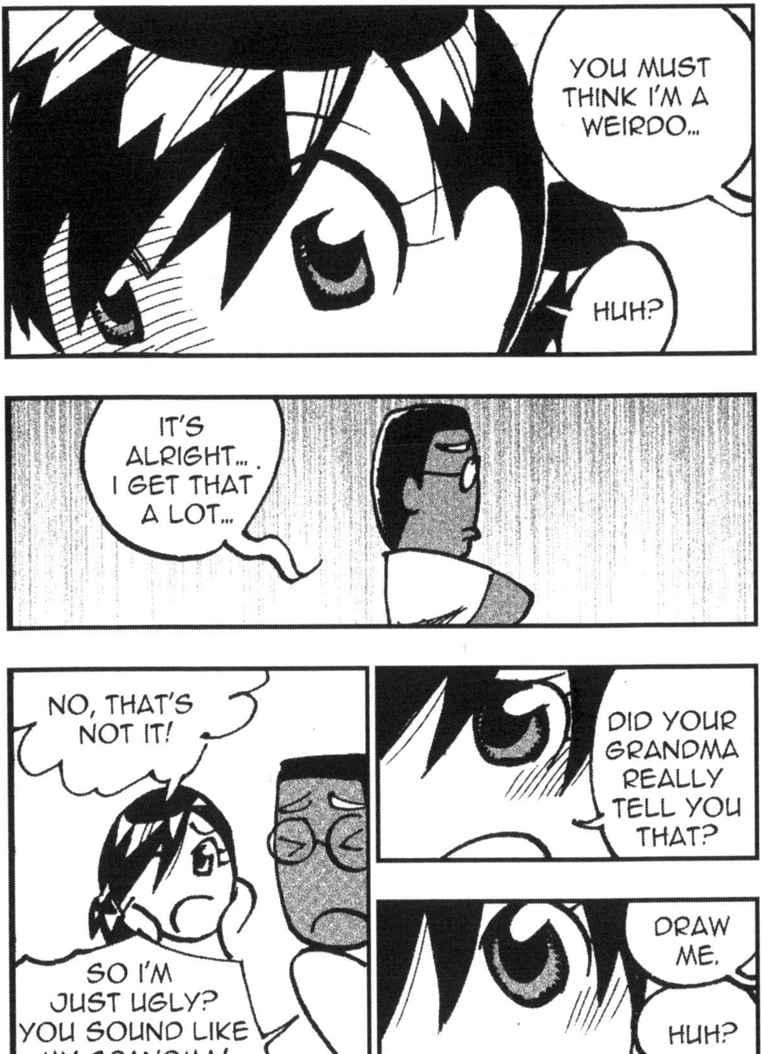
YOU MUST THINK I'M A WEIRDO...
HUH?
IT'S ALRIGHT... I GET THAT A LOT...
NO, THAT'S NOT IT!
SO I'M JUST UGLY? YOU SOUND LIKE MY GRANDMA!
DID YOUR GRANDMA REALLY TELL YOU THAT?
DRAW ME.
HUH?

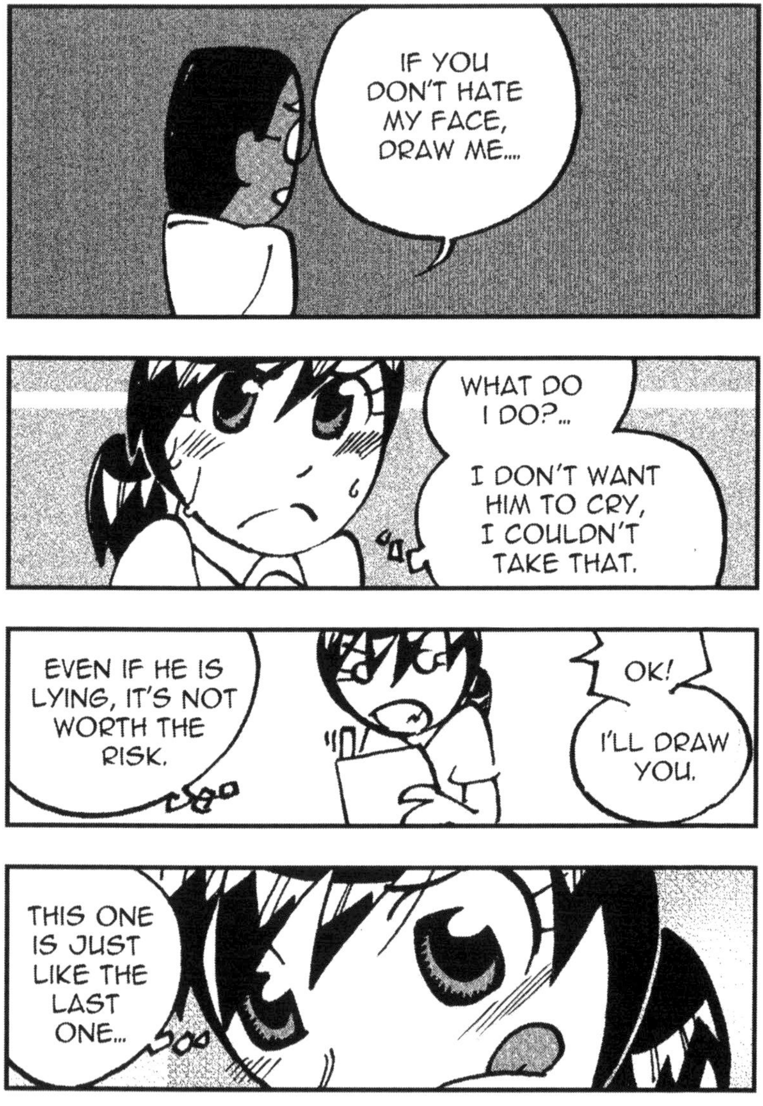
IF YOU DON'T HATE MY FACE, DRAW ME....
WHAT DO I DO?...
I DON'T WANT HIM TO CRY, I COULDN'T TAKE THAT.
EVEN IF HE IS LYING, IT'S NOT WORTH THE RISK.
OK!
I'LL DRAW YOU.
THIS ONE IS JUST LIKE THE LAST ONE...

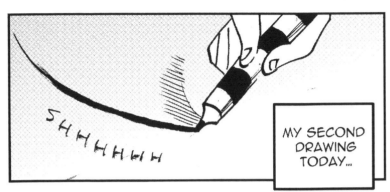

MY SECOND DRAWING TODAY...

THIS ONE WILL BE DIFFERENT ...

FOR TWO REASONS ...

SOME-ONE'S FEELINGS ARE ON THE LINE, AND...

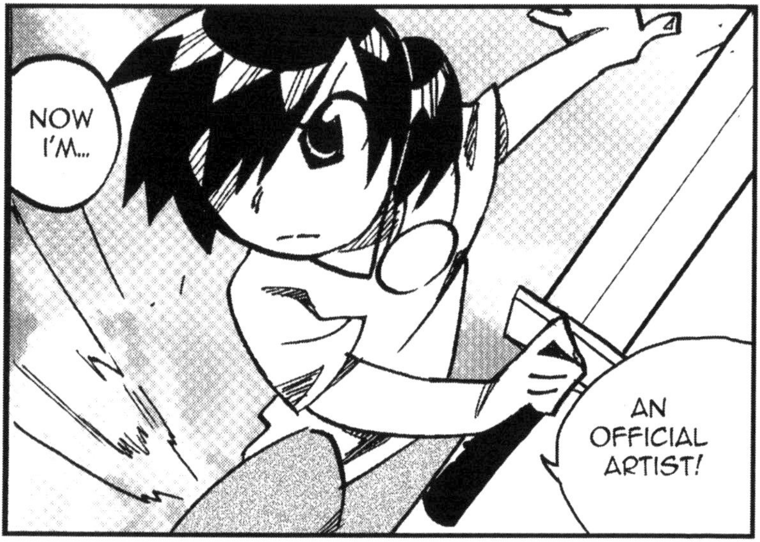
NOW I'M...
AN OFFICIAL ARTIST!

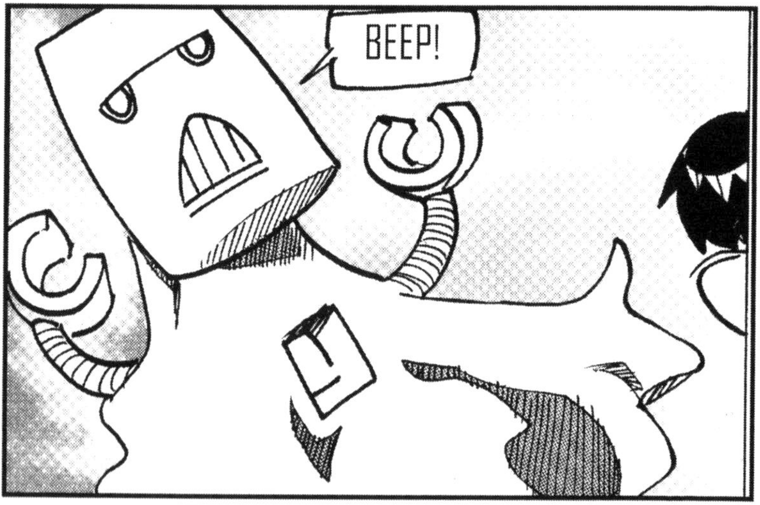
BEEP!

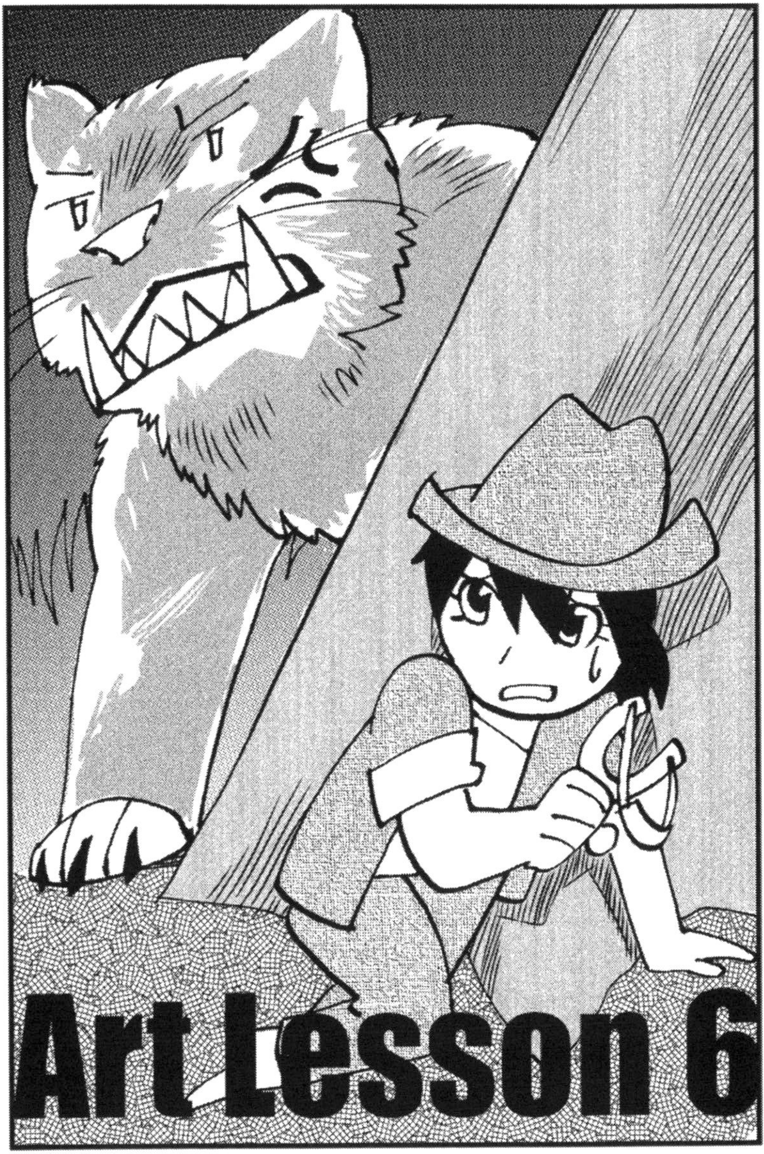
Art Lesson 6

IN ART AS IN LOVE, INSTINCT IS ENOUGH.
-ANATOLE FRANCE

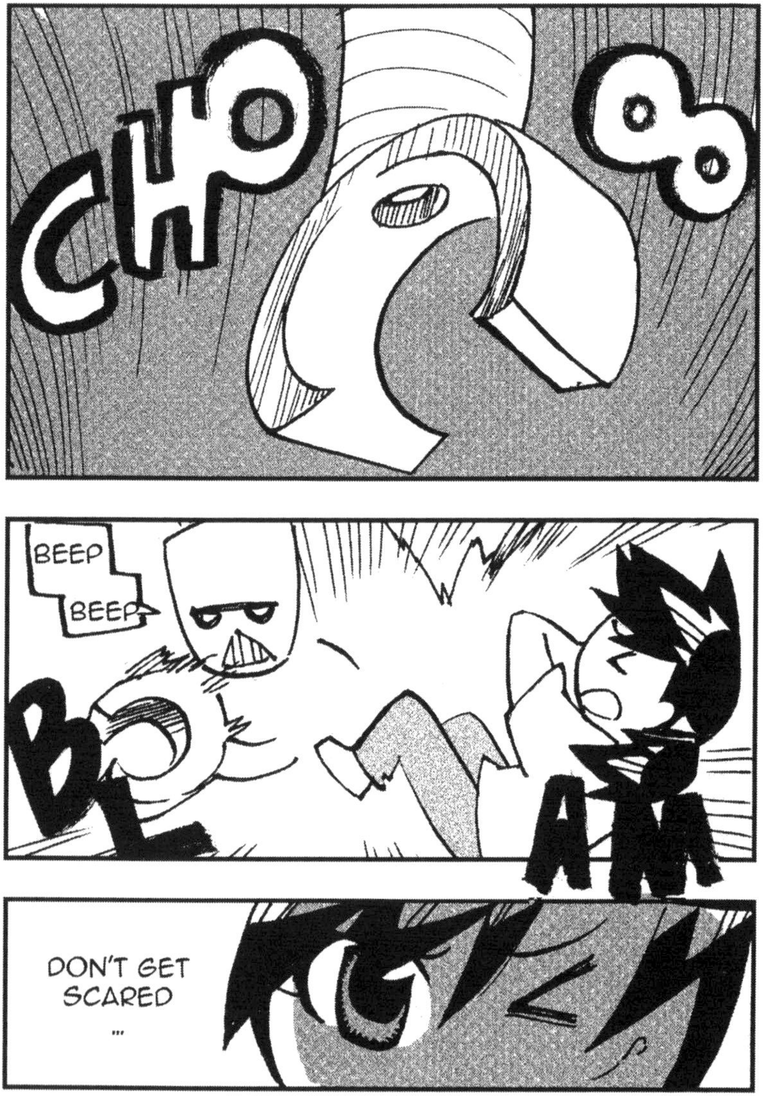
CHO
BEEP
BEEP
BL
AM
DON'T GET SCARED
...

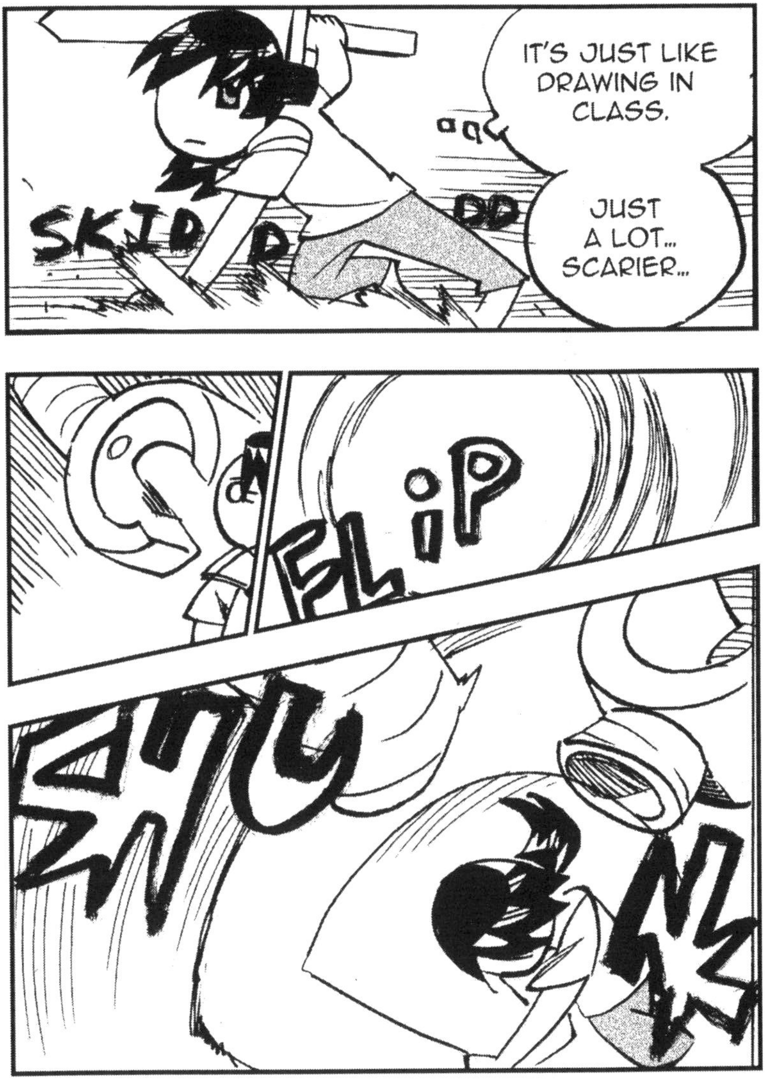
SKID
D
DD
IT'S JUST LIKE DRAWING IN CLASS.
JUST A LOT... SCARIER...
FLIP

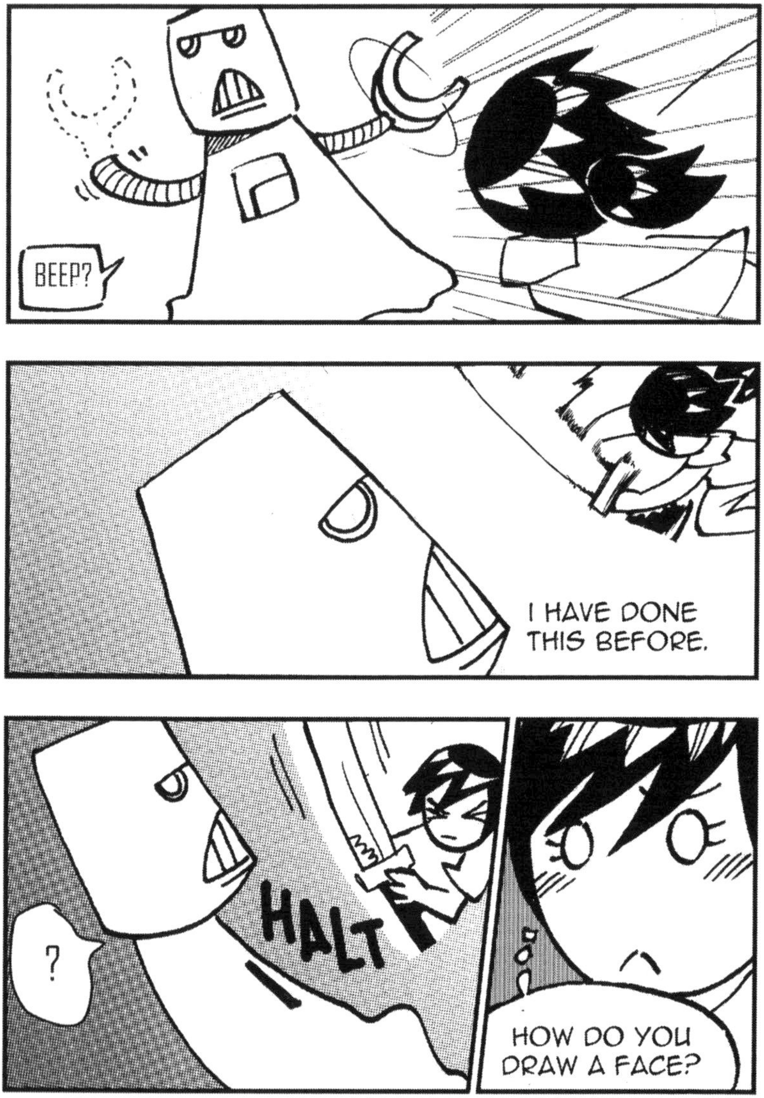
BEEP?
I HAVE DONE THIS BEFORE.
HALT
?
HOW DO YOU DRAW A FACE?

CH
NEVER DREW A REAL FACE BEFORE...
ACK!
BLAM
WHAT'S WRONG, FRAN?

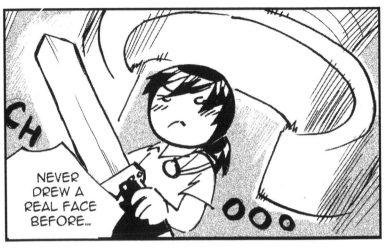

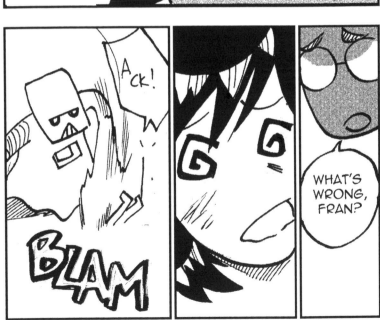

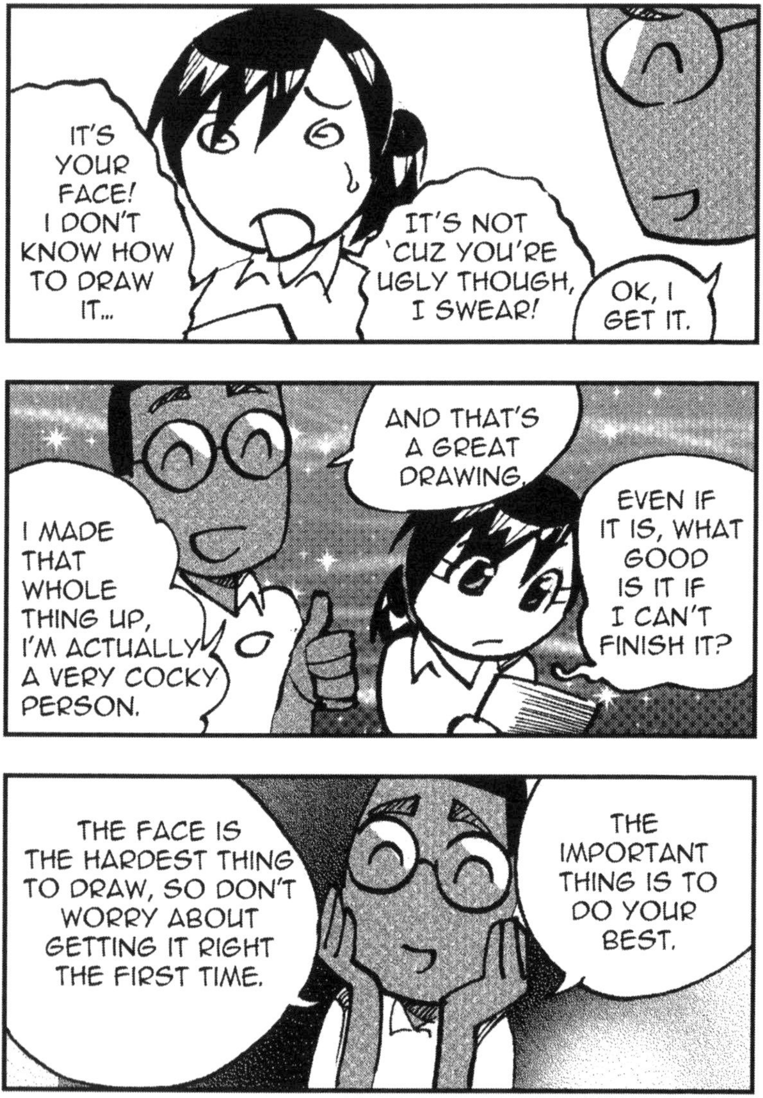
IT'S YOUR FACE! I DON'T KNOW HOW TO DRAW IT...
IT'S NOT 'CUZ YOU'RE UGLY THOUGH, I SWEAR!
OK, I GET IT.
AND THAT'S A GREAT DRAWING.
I MADE THAT WHOLE THING UP, I'M ACTUALLY A VERY COCKY PERSON.
EVEN IF IT IS, WHAT GOOD IS IT IF I CAN'T FINISH IT?
THE FACE IS THE HARDEST THING TO DRAW, SO DON'T WORRY ABOUT GETTING IT RIGHT THE FIRST TIME.
THE IMPORTANT THING IS TO DO YOUR BEST.

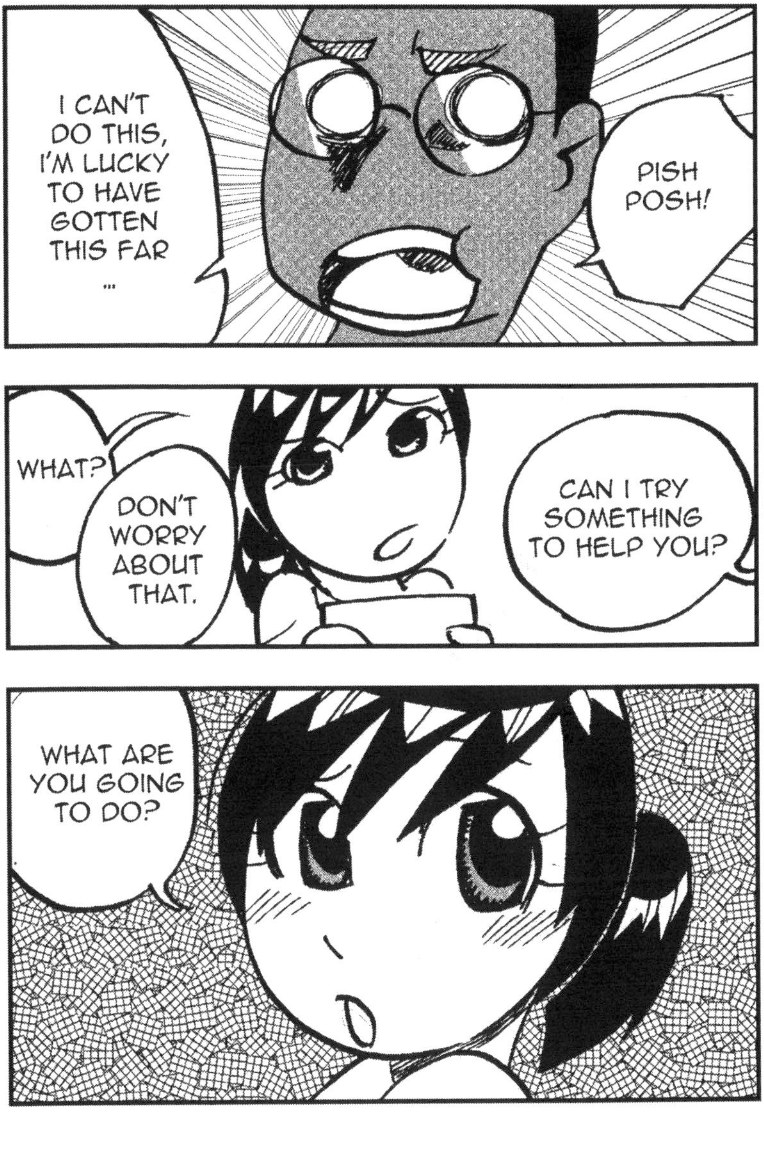
I CAN'T DO THIS, I'M LUCKY TO HAVE GOTTEN THIS FAR ...
PISH POSH!
WHAT?
DON'T WORRY ABOUT THAT.
CAN I TRY SOMETHING TO HELP YOU?
WHAT ARE YOU GOING TO DO?

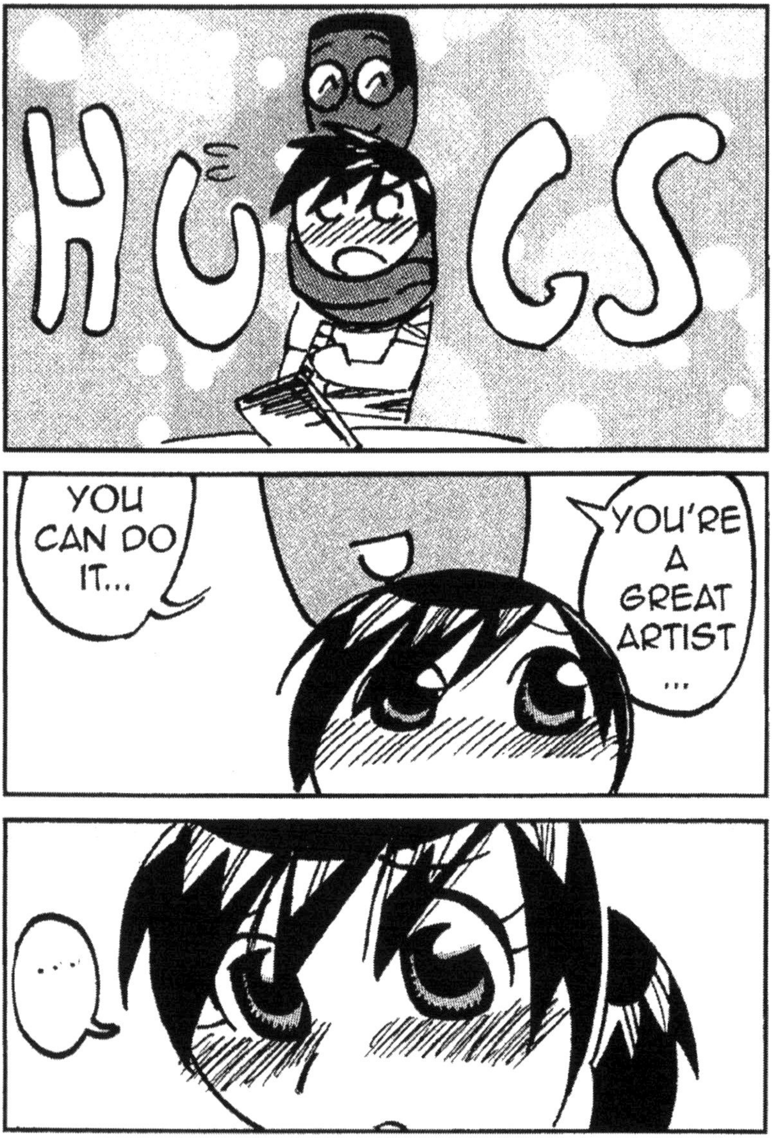
HUGS
YOU CAN DO IT...
YOU'RE A GREAT ARTIST ...
...

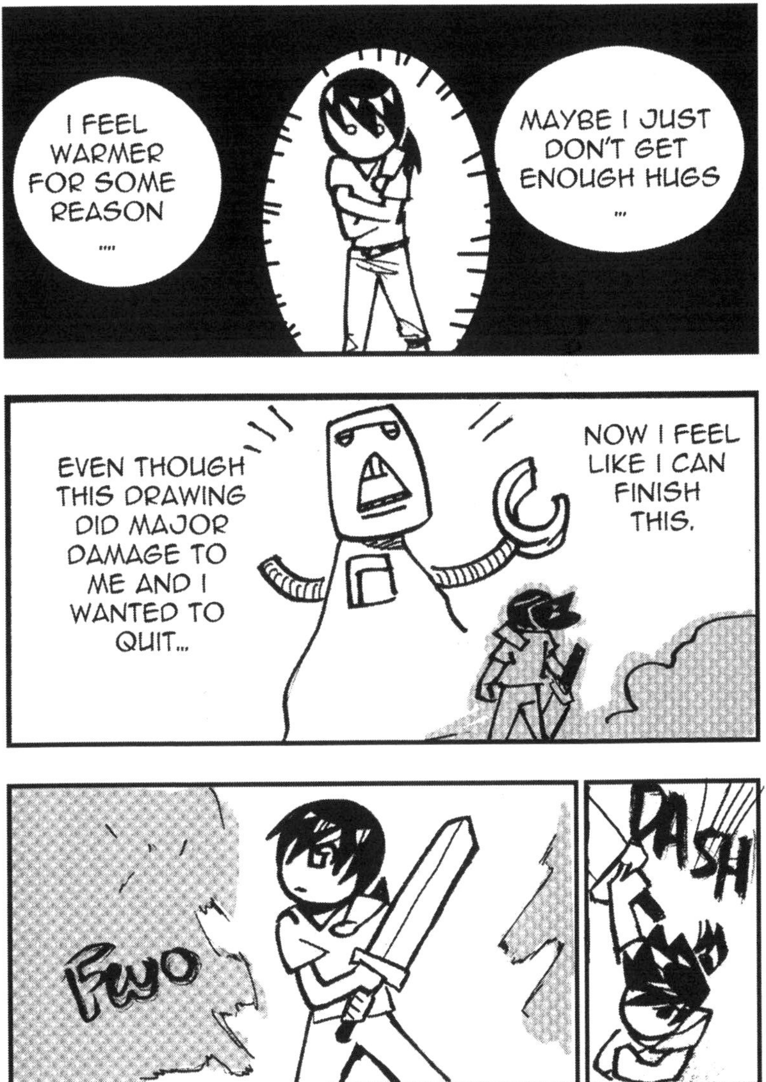
I FEEL WARMER FOR SOME REASON ....
MAYBE I JUST DON'T GET ENOUGH HUGS ...
EVEN THOUGH THIS DRAWING DID MAJOR DAMAGE TO ME AND I WANTED TO QUIT...
NOW I FEEL LIKE I CAN FINISH THIS.
FWO
DASH

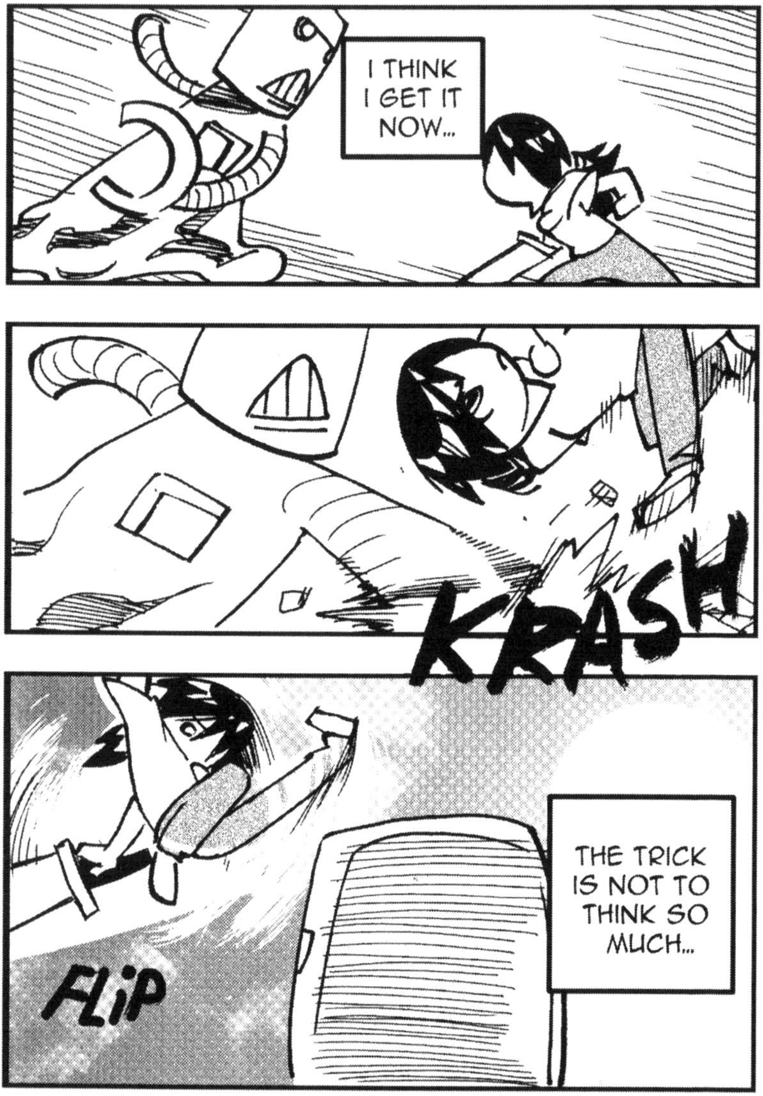
I THINK I GET IT NOW...
KRASH
FLiP
THE TRICK IS NOT TO THINK SO MUCH...

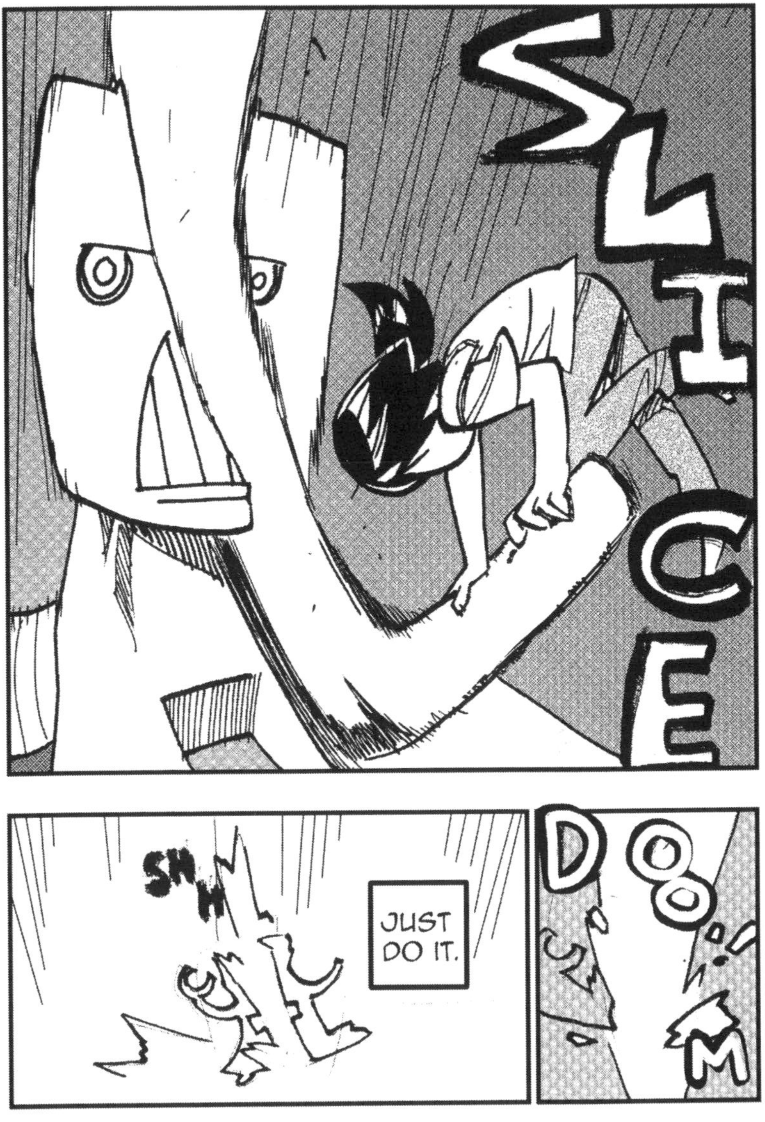
SLICE
JUST
DO IT.

YOU DID IT!
YEA... LOOKS LIKE IT.
SO, IS HUGGING YOUR SPECIAL POWER?
UMM, WHAT DO YOU MEAN?
I JUST GIVE GOOD HUGS IS ALL,
BUT I GUESS YOU COULD CALL IT A SPECIAL POWER.
OH NO, WHAT I MEANT WAS...
I'M SORRY I KNOW THAT MUST SOUND CRAZY.

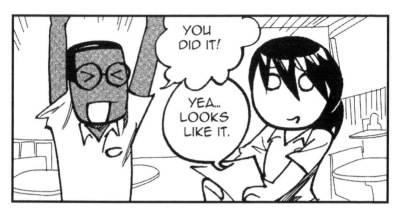

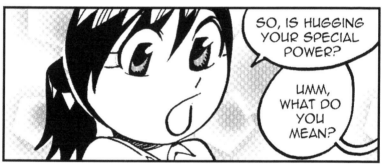

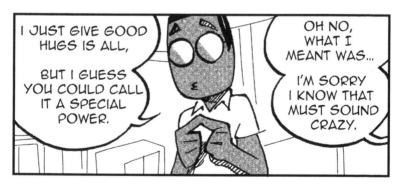

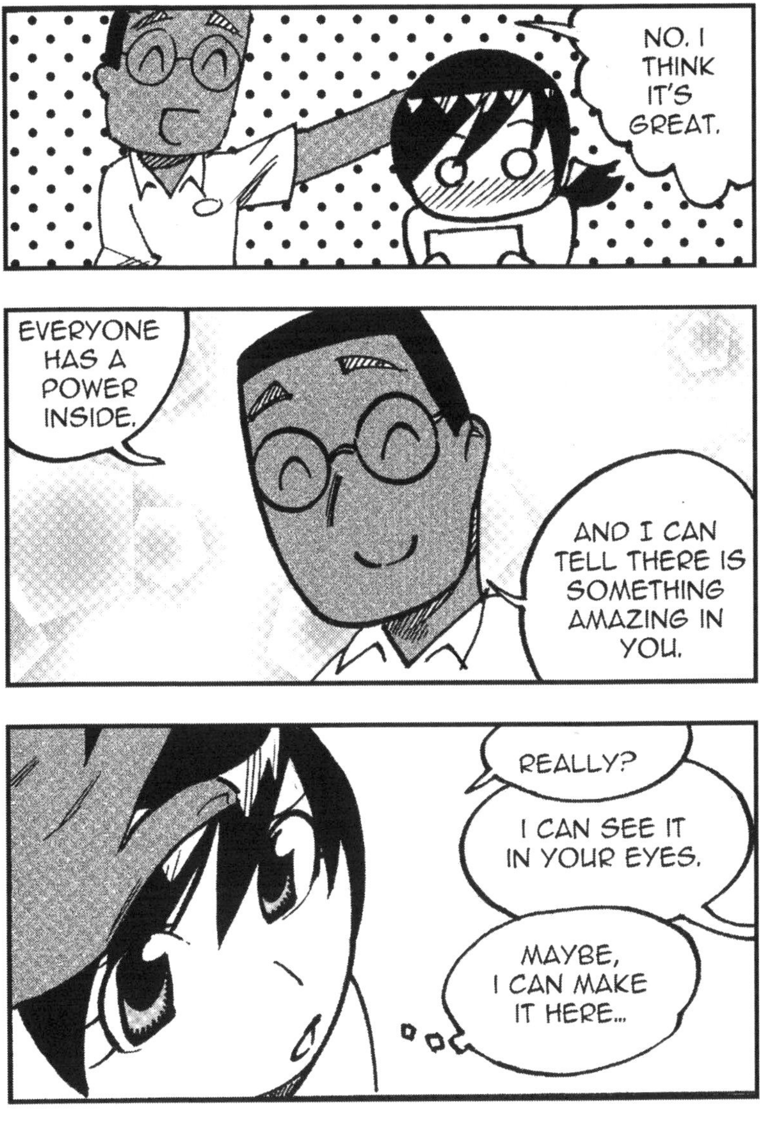
NO. I THINK IT'S GREAT.
EVERYONE HAS A POWER INSIDE.
AND I CAN TELL THERE IS SOMETHING AMAZING IN YOU.
REALLY?
I CAN SEE IT IN YOUR EYES.
MAYBE, I CAN MAKE IT HERE...

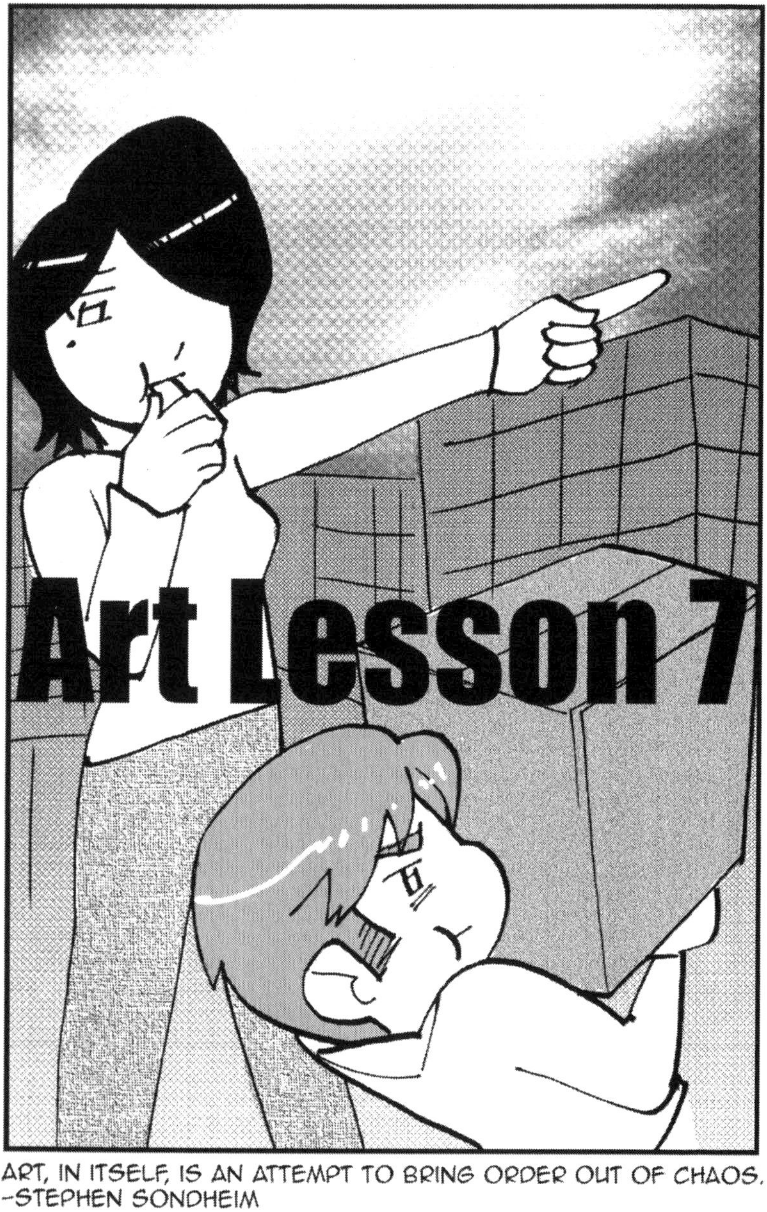
Art Lesson 7

ART, IN ITSELF, IS AN ATTEMPT TO BRING ORDER OUT OF CHAOS.
-STEPHEN SONDHEIM

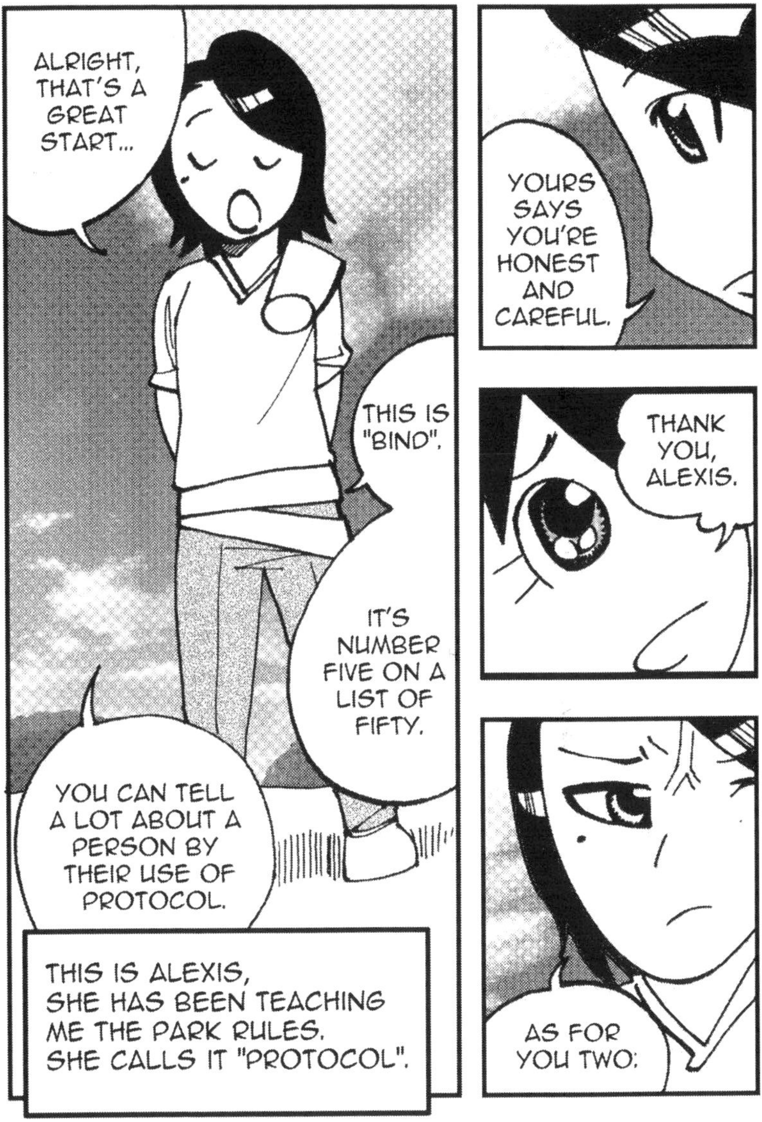
ALRIGHT, THAT'S A GREAT START...
THIS IS "BIND".
IT'S NUMBER FIVE ON A LIST OF FIFTY.
YOU CAN TELL A LOT ABOUT A PERSON BY THEIR USE OF PROTOCOL.
THIS IS ALEXIS, SHE HAS BEEN TEACHING ME THE PARK RULES. SHE CALLS IT "PROTOCOL".
YOURS SAYS YOU'RE HONEST AND CAREFUL.
THANK YOU, ALEXIS.
AS FOR YOU TWO:

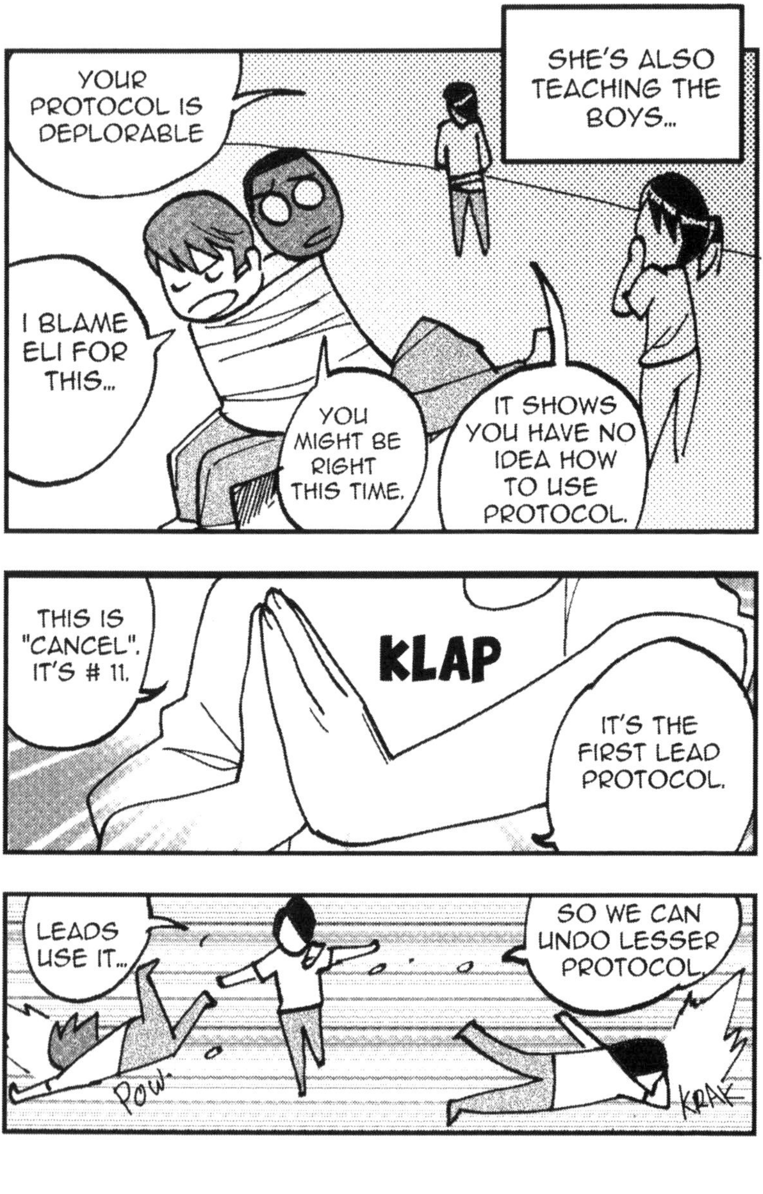
SHE'S ALSO TEACHING THE BOYS...
YOUR PROTOCOL IS DEPLORABLE
I BLAME ELI FOR THIS...
YOU MIGHT BE RIGHT THIS TIME.
IT SHOWS YOU HAVE NO IDEA HOW TO USE PROTOCOL.
THIS IS "CANCEL". IT'S # 11.
KLAP
IT'S THE FIRST LEAD PROTOCOL.
LEADS USE IT...
SO WE CAN UNDO LESSER PROTOCOL.
POW
KRAK

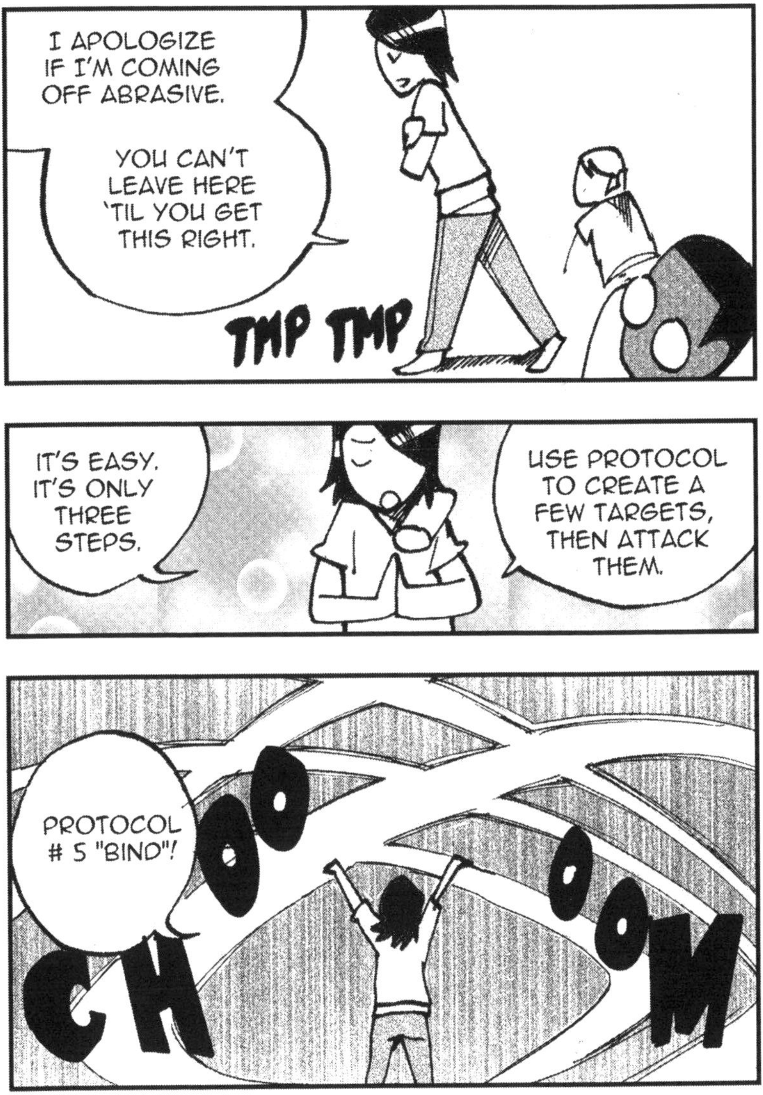
I APOLOGIZE IF I'M COMING OFF ABRASIVE.
YOU CAN'T LEAVE HERE 'TIL YOU GET THIS RIGHT.
TMP TMP
IT'S EASY. IT'S ONLY THREE STEPS.
USE PROTOCOL TO CREATE A FEW TARGETS, THEN ATTACK THEM.
PROTOCOL # 5 "BIND"!
CHOOOOOOM

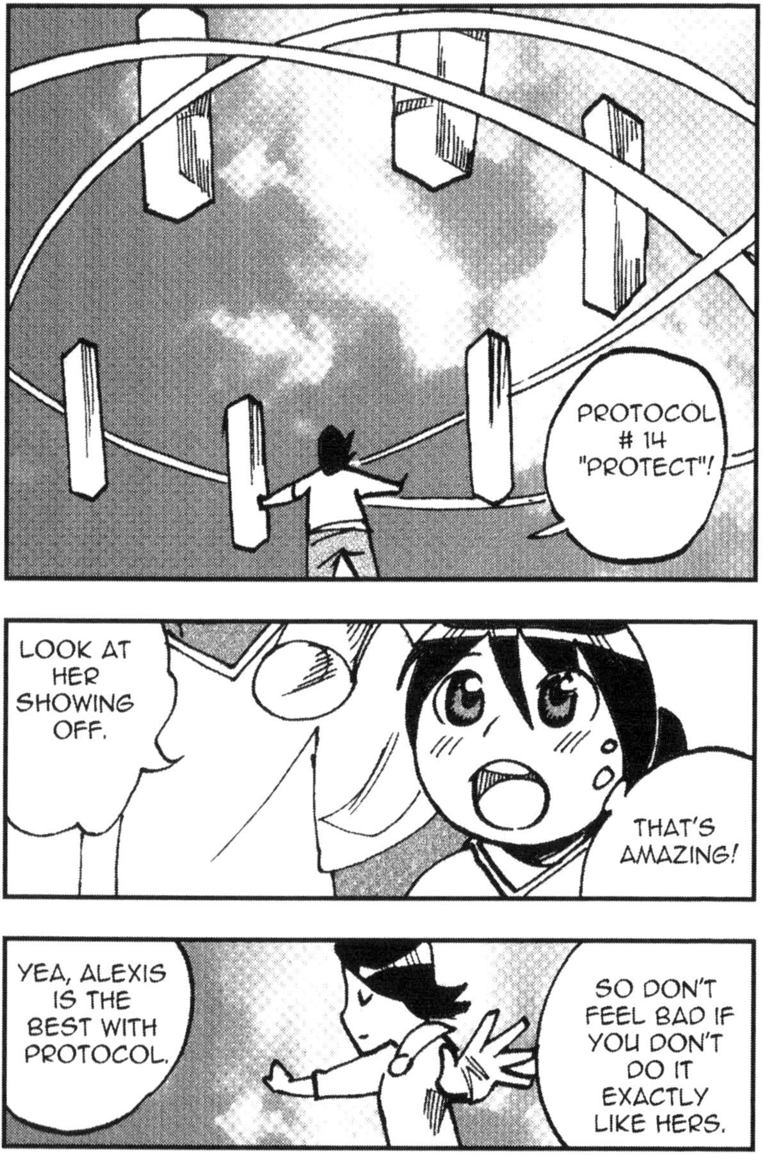
PROTOCOL # 14 "PROTECT"!
LOOK AT HER SHOWING OFF.
THAT'S AMAZING!
YEA, ALEXIS IS THE BEST WITH PROTOCOL.
SO DON'T FEEL BAD IF YOU DON'T DO IT EXACTLY LIKE HERS.

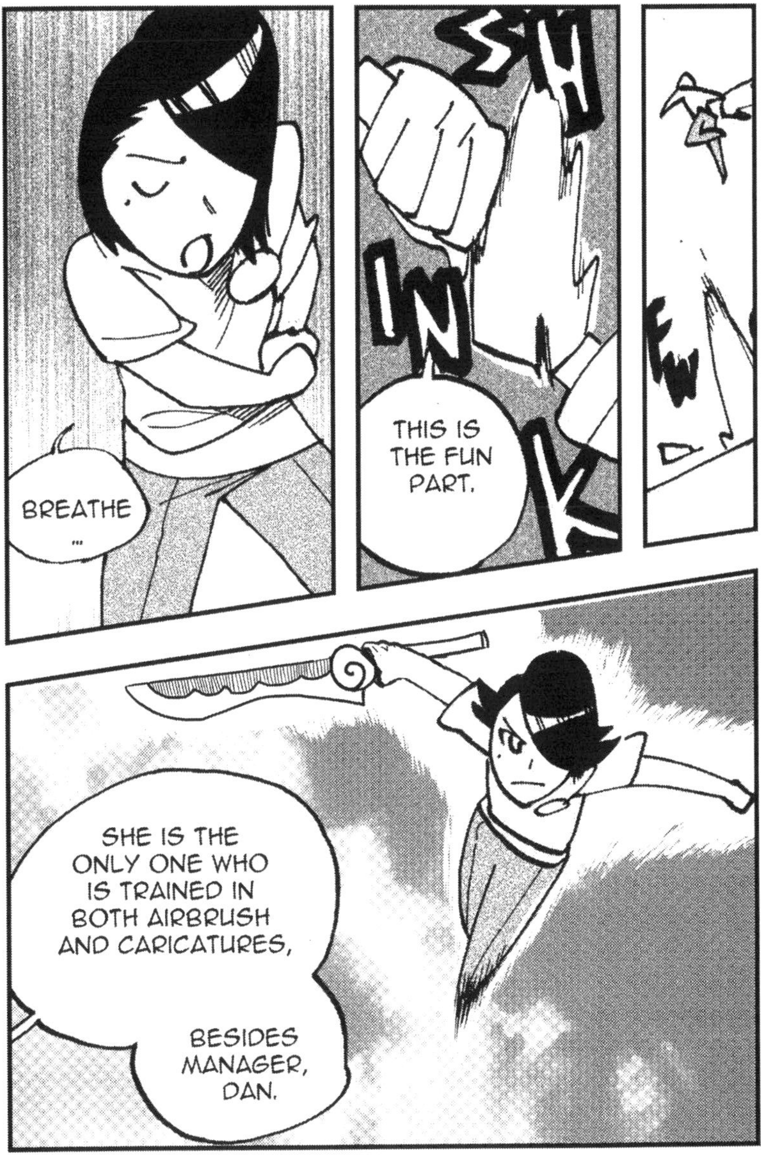
BREATHE ...
SHINK
THIS IS THE FUN PART.
SHE IS THE ONLY ONE WHO IS TRAINED IN BOTH AIRBRUSH AND CARICATURES,
BESIDES MANAGER, DAN.

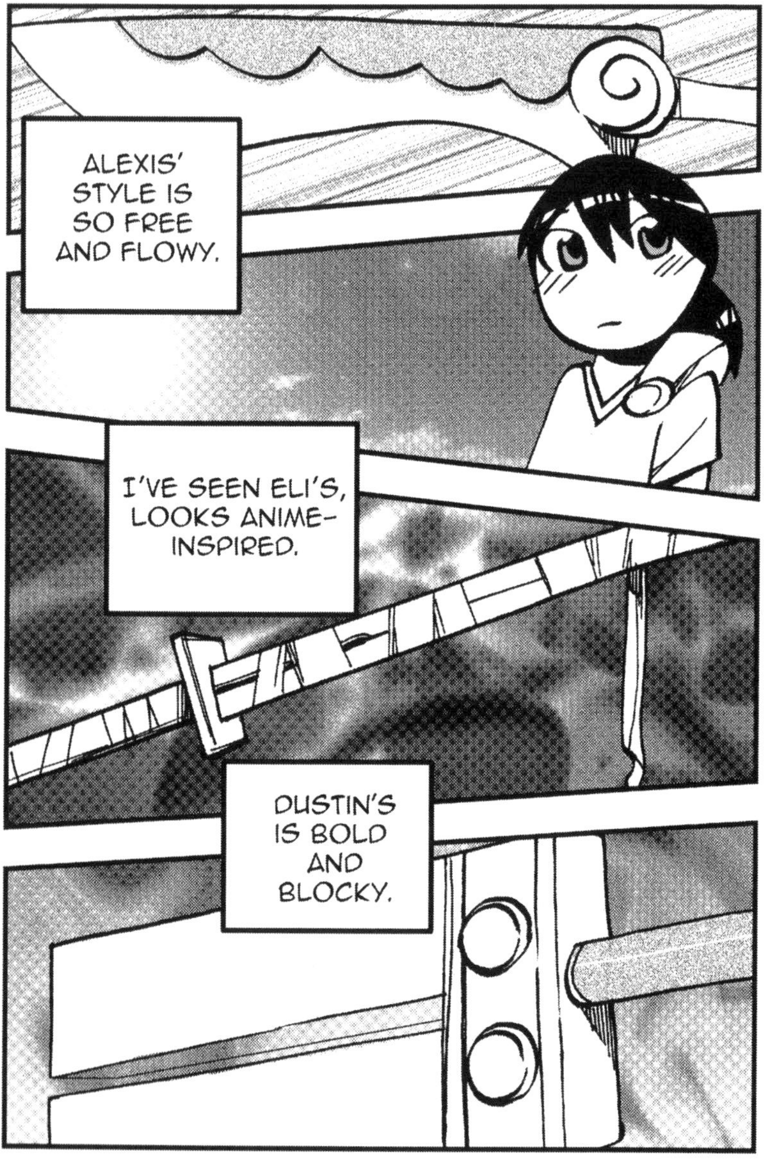
ALEXIS' STYLE IS SO FREE AND FLOWY.
I'VE SEEN ELI'S, LOOKS ANIME-INSPIRED.
DUSTIN'S IS BOLD AND BLOCKY.

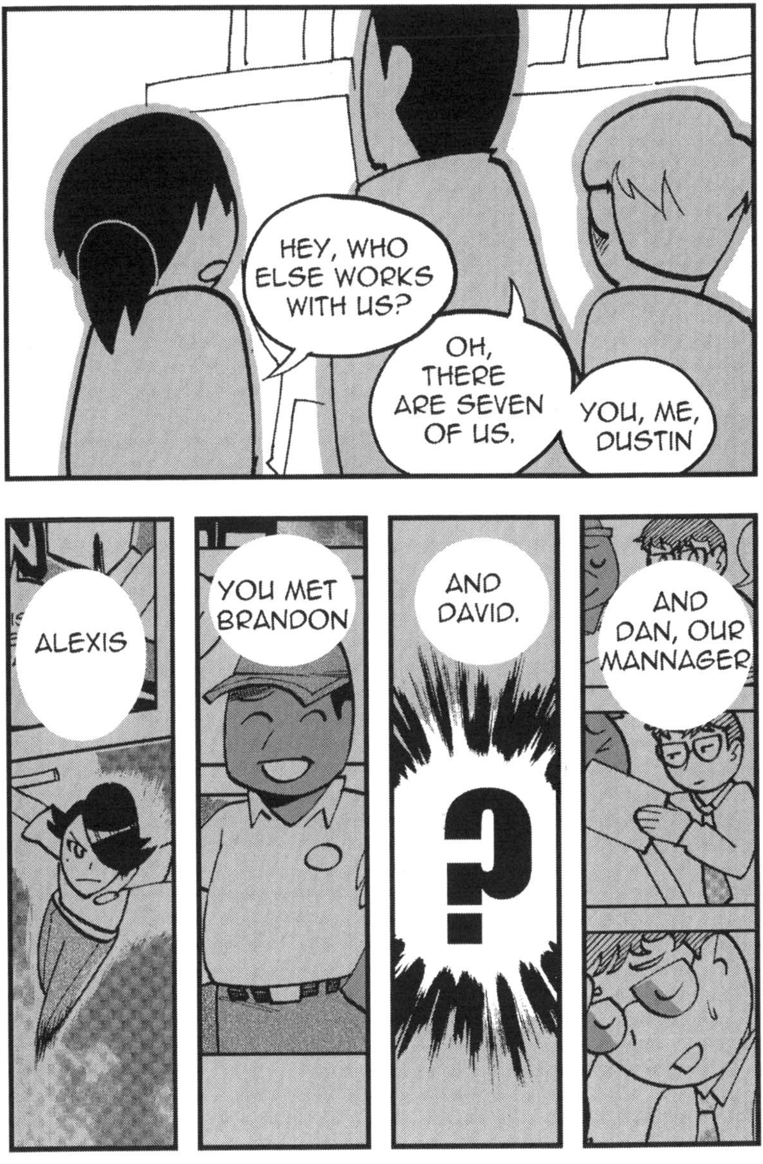
HEY, WHO ELSE WORKS WITH US?
OH, THERE ARE SEVEN OF US.
YOU, ME, DUSTIN
ALEXIS
YOU MET BRANDON
AND DAVID.
?
AND DAN, OUR MANNAGER

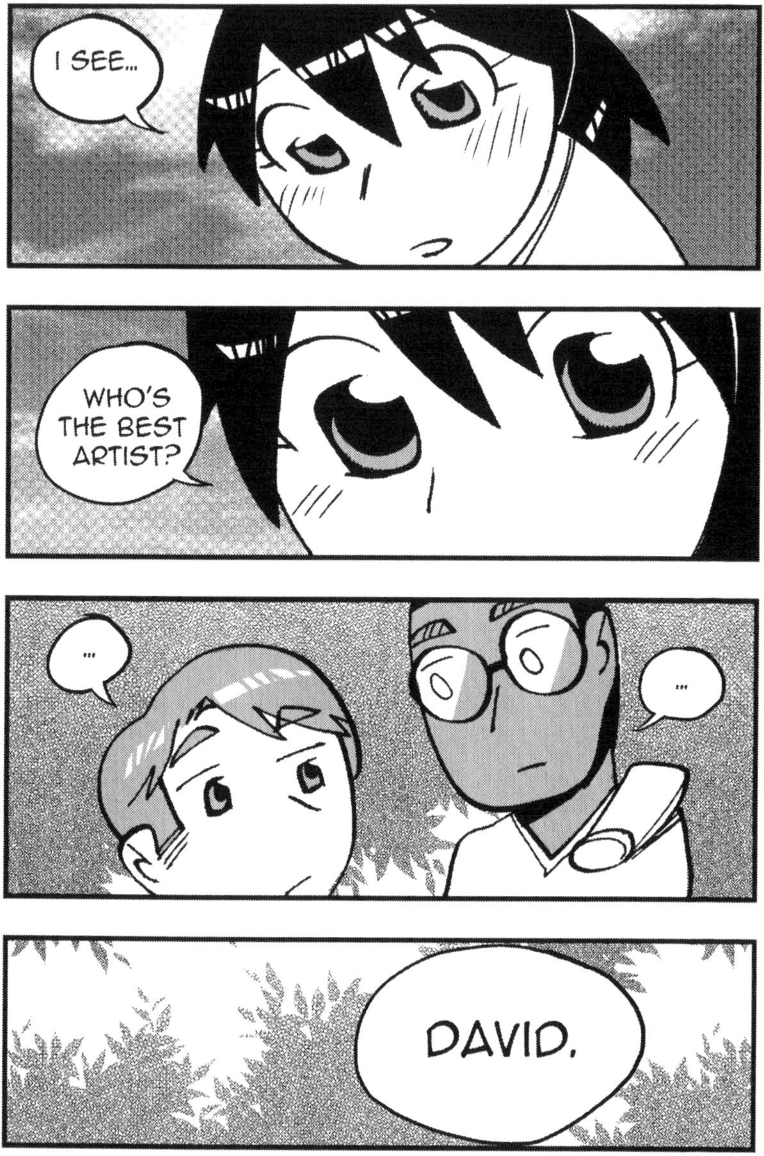
I SEE...
WHO'S THE BEST ARTIST?
...
...
DAVID.

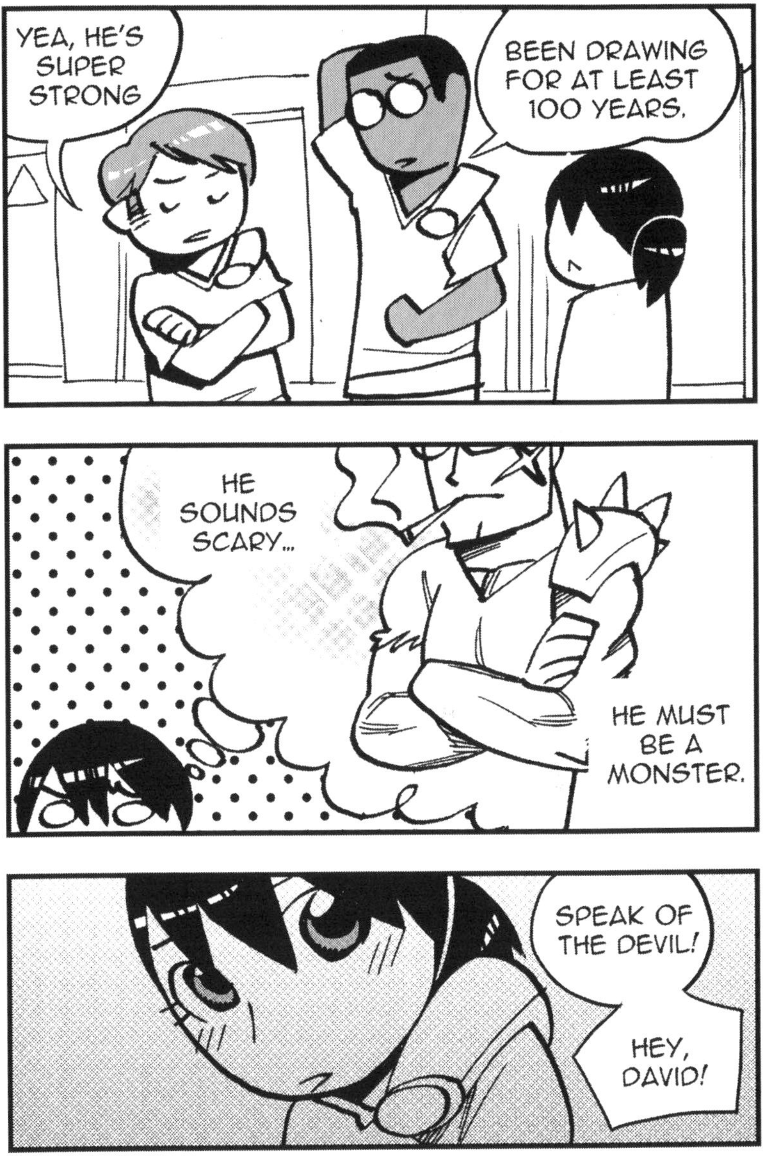
YEA, HE'S SUPER STRONG
BEEN DRAWING FOR AT LEAST 100 YEARS.
HE SOUNDS SCARY...
HE MUST BE A MONSTER.
SPEAK OF THE DEVIL!
HEY, DAVID!

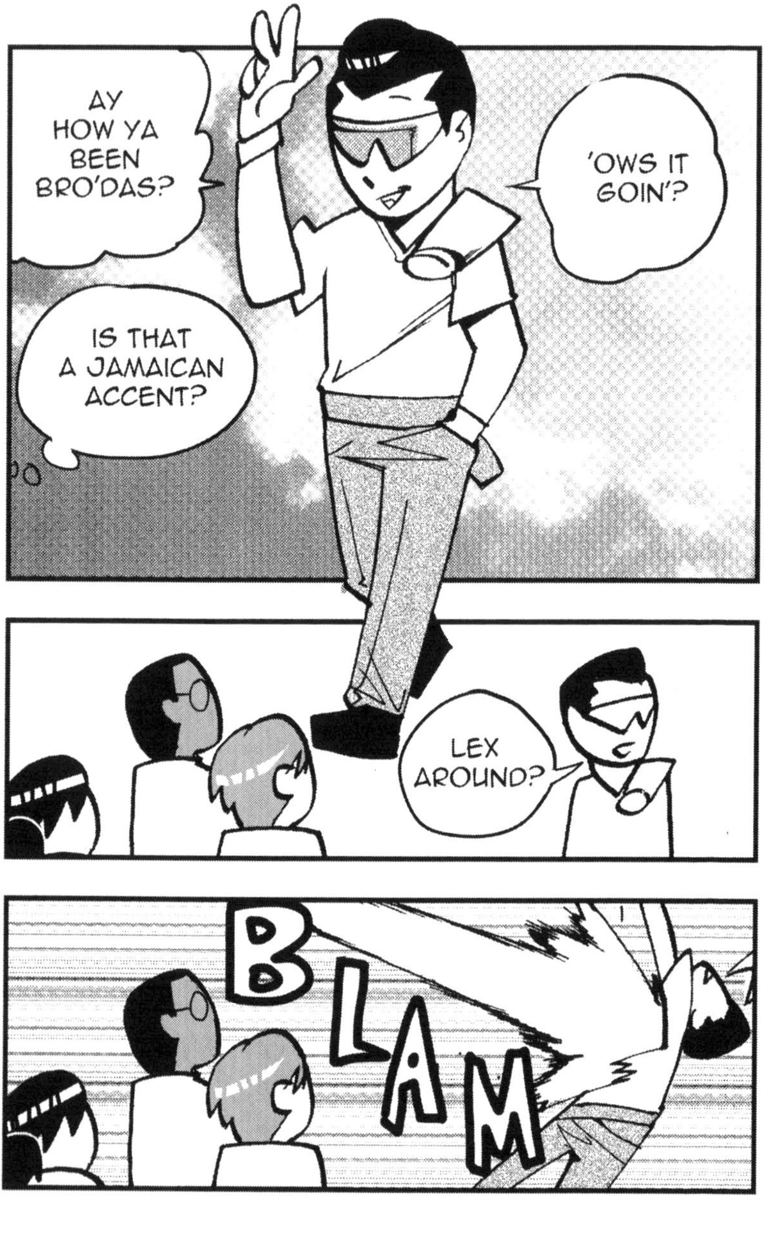
AY HOW YA BEEN BRO'DAS?
'OWS IT GOIN'?
IS THAT A JAMAICAN ACCENT?
LEX AROUND?
BLAM

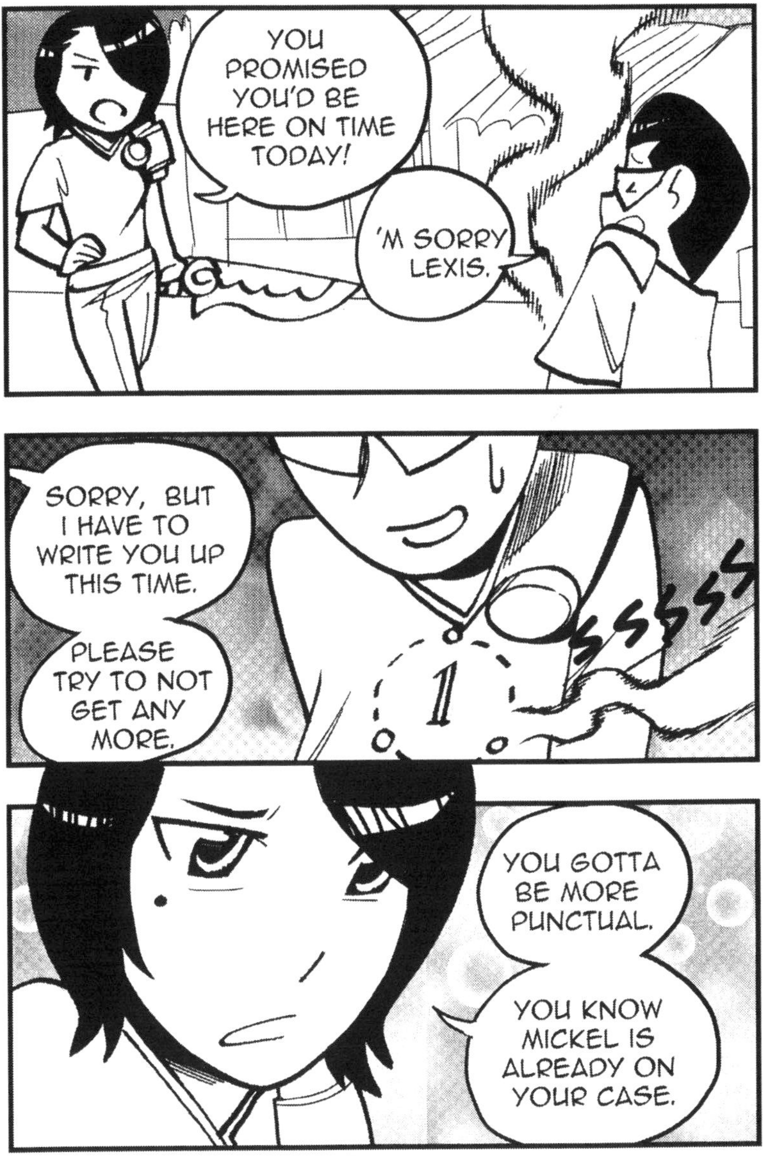
YOU PROMISED YOU'D BE HERE ON TIME TODAY!
'M SORRY LEXIS.
SORRY, BUT I HAVE TO WRITE YOU UP THIS TIME.
PLEASE TRY TO NOT GET ANY MORE.
1
YOU GOTTA BE MORE PUNCTUAL.
YOU KNOW MICKEL IS ALREADY ON YOUR CASE.

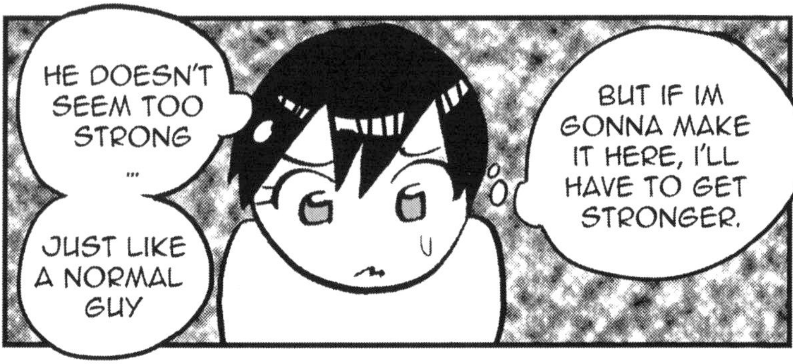
HE DOESN'T SEEM TOO STRONG ...
JUST LIKE A NORMAL GUY
BUT IF IM GONNA MAKE IT HERE, I'LL HAVE TO GET STRONGER.

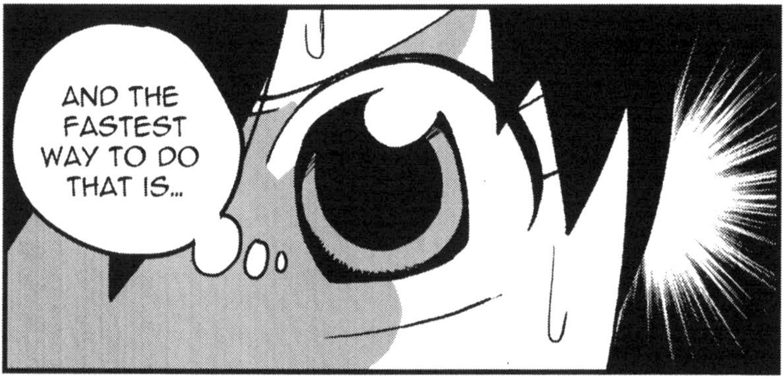
AND THE FASTEST WAY TO DO THAT IS...

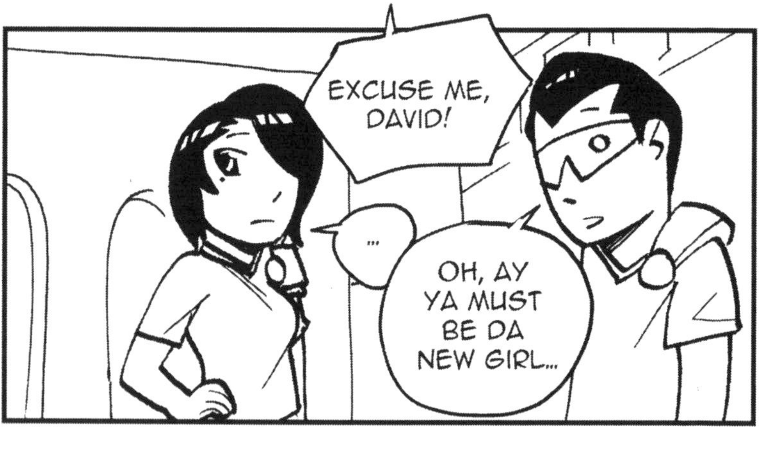
EXCUSE ME, DAVID!
...
OH, AY YA MUST BE DA NEW GIRL...

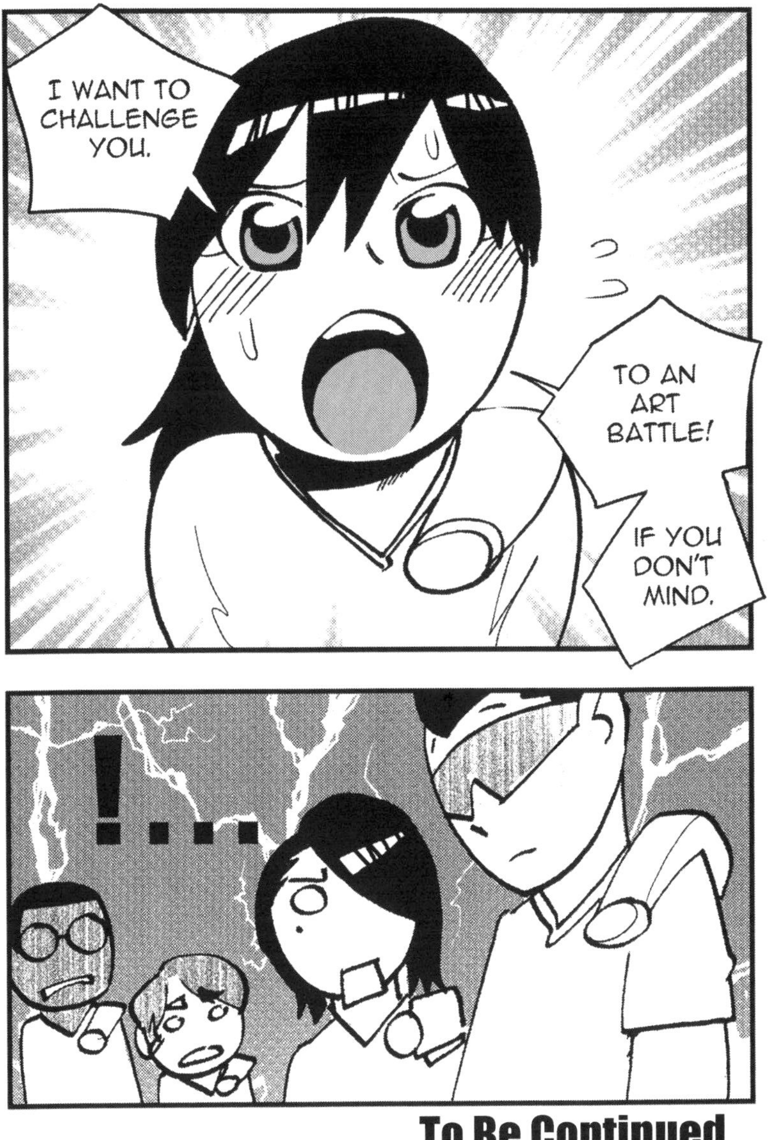
I WANT TO CHALLENGE YOU.
TO AN ART BATTLE!
IF YOU DON'T MIND.
!...

To Be Continued...

Action land Book 2 coming soon

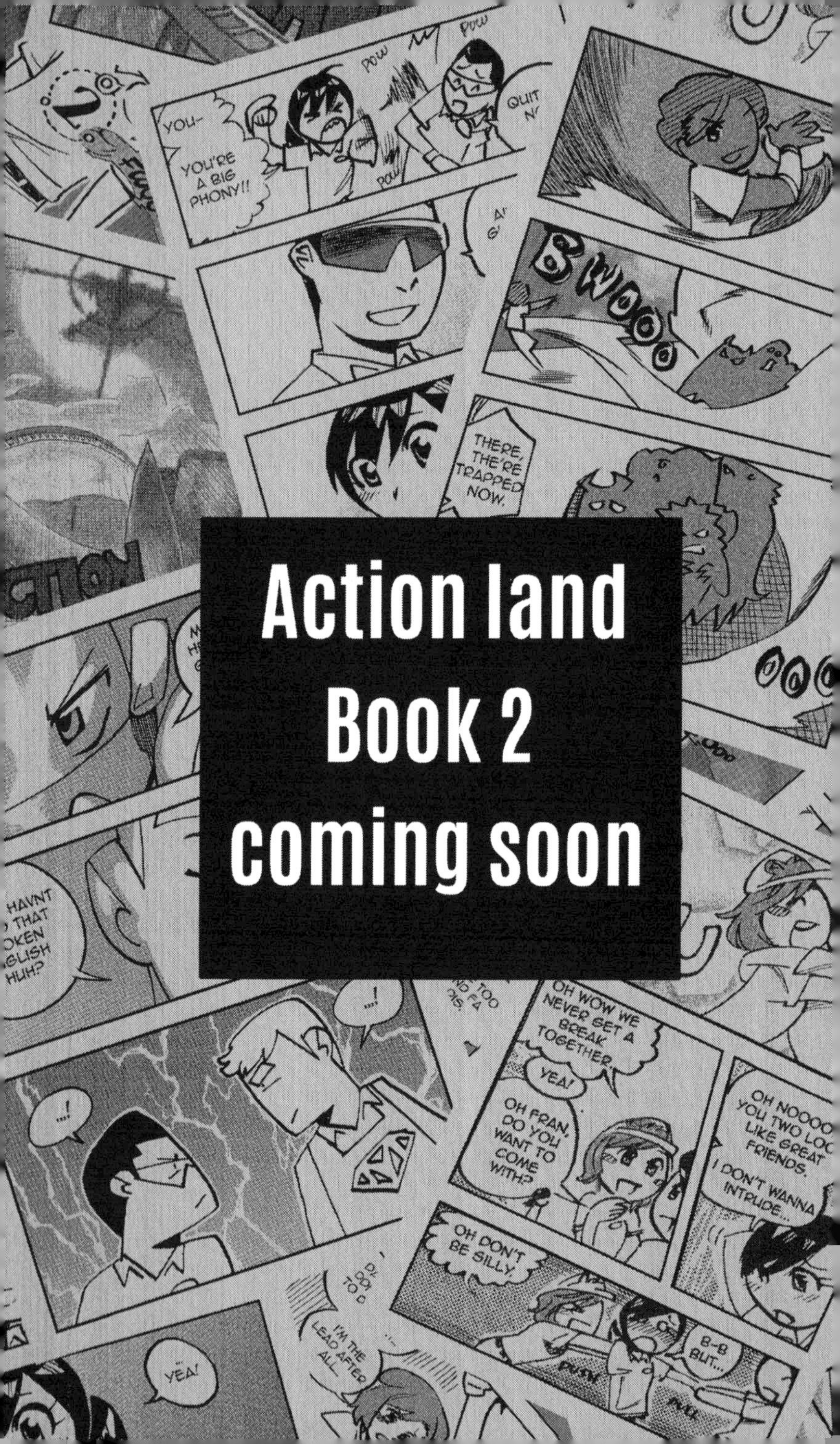
YOU–
YOU'RE A BIG PHONY!!
POW
POW
QUIT N'
THERE, THE'RE TRAPPED NOW.
OH WOW WE NEVER GET A BREAK TOGETHER
YEA!
OH FRAN, DO YOU WANT TO COME WITH?
I DON'T WANNA INTRUDE...
OH DON'T BE SILLY.
I'M THE LEAD AFTER ALL...
B-B BUT...
PUSH
PULL
YEA!

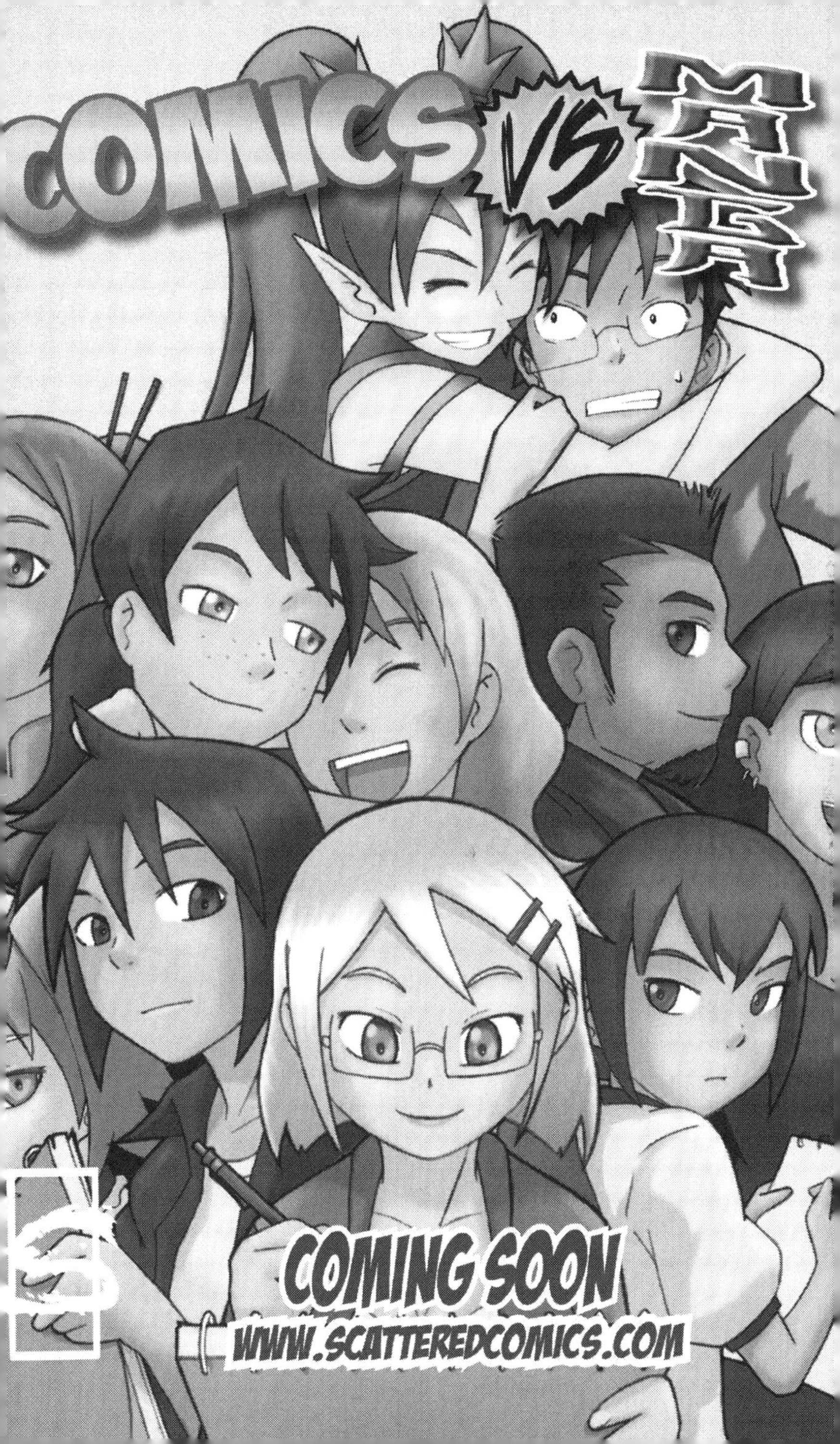
COMICS VS MANGA
COMING SOON
WWW.SCATTEREDCOMICS.COM

THANK YOU FOR READING MY FIRST BOOK!

IT MEANS THE WORLD TO ME. I HOPE IT MADE YOU
GIGGLE TO YOURSELF.
ACTION LAND HAS BEEN IN THE WORKS SINCE 2009,
 WHEN I STARTED WORKING AT SIX FLAGS. ALTHOUGH
I AM ARROGANT ENOUGH TO PUT MYSELF IN THE BOOK,
I THOUGHT IT WOULD BE MORE INTERESTING IF I DIDN'T
MAKE MYSELF THE MAIN CHARACTER. IN FACT MY
CHARACTER (ELI) WILL SLOWLY BECOME ONE OF THE
ANTAGONISTS (DRAMATIC MUSIC).

I HAVE NOTICED THAT ACTION LAND DOESN'T HAVE AS
MANY FANS AS MY OTHER STORIES BUT THE PEOPLE
WHO DO LIKE IT, REALLY LIKE IT. I THINK IT'S BECAUSE
THEY CAN SEE THE POTENTIAL IN IT THAT I SEE.
ACTION LAND IS GOING PLACES, YOU JUST WAIT!
I HAVE ALL 10 BOOKS ALREADY ROUGHED OUT, AND
EVERY BOOK GETS BETTER AND BETTER, AND I CAN'T
WAIT TO SHOW YOU.

ASIDE FROM THAT, I'M NOT REALLY SURE WHAT ELSE
TO SAY HERE. IF YOU HAVE ANY QUESTIONS, OR JUST
WANT TO TALK TO ME, SEND ME AN EMAIL AT
SLIMCOMICBOOKS@GMAIL.COM AND WE CAN CHAT.

THANKS AGAIN FOR READING!

ELI

Made in the USA
San Bernardino, CA
12 September 2017